# *You Have a Ministry*

First Church of the Brethren
1340 Forge Road
Carlisle, Pennsylvania 17013

# YOU
## HAVE A
## MINISTRY

*Christian Laymen Are Called to Serve*

## By R. Eugene Sterner

WARNER PRESS          ANDERSON, INDIANA

## ACKNOWLEDGMENTS

Scripture quotations marked "Phillips" are from The New Testament in Modern English, translated by J. B. Phillips and copyright, 1958, by J. B. Phillips. Used by permission of The Macmillan Company, New York. Scripture quotations marked "NEB" are copyright, 1961, by the Delegates of the Oxford University Press and the Syndics of the Cambridge University Press and are used by permission. Scripture quotations marked "RSV" are from the Revised Standard Version of the Holy Bible, copyright, 1952, by the Division of Christian Education, NCCCUSA, and are used by permission. Scripture quotations marked "Weymouth" are from The New Testament in Modern Speech by Richard Francis Weymouth, copyright, 1937, by Harper and Row, Publishers, Inc., and used by permission. Scripture quotations marked "Moffatt" are from A New Translation of the Bible by Moffatt, copyright, 1935, by Harper and Row, Publishers, Inc., and used by permission. Unmarked passages are from the King James Version of the Bible. Quotations from other material are acknowledged in footnotes.

# Preface

This book is addressed to the layman—businessman, carpenter, lawyer, doctor, crane operator, engineer, teacher, or laborer. It comes from an ordained minister who feels that if the church is to get out beyond its cloister into everyday vocational and family life, the ministry must be shared by all Christians.

If some of us have had special training and discipline in the field of theology and religion, or if our job is in some way different from that of others, we want it to give us greater perspective and help us appreciate more deeply all aspects of life, rather than allow it to crowd us into a narrow niche, thinking and speaking a language that the average man doesn't understand or appreciate.

The church does need spiritual renewal. It needs a fresh relevance to life as the average or typical person lives and experiences it. There is a widespread sense of need to rediscover the nature of the church as "the whole people of God" and to give it expression, even rethinking our patterns of church work and organization. We are hearing and reading a great deal about the theology of the church and of the laity—and these two considerations belong together.

This is not intended to be a theology, however. It is intended to explore the ministry of the layman himself, as much as possible, from his viewpoint. It is more practical than scholarly.

I am indebted to many writers and teachers, some of whom are indicated in the footnotes, and also to my faithful and diligent secretary, Mrs. Lois Forsberg, who has performed her own ministry of helpfulness with a sense of calling and mission under God.

It is my fond hope that you who will read these pages may find reward and meaning in your everyday life and work and that you will discover that peculiar ministry which is yours and yours alone.                    —R. Eugene Sterner

# Contents

*The church is a ministry,*
*not an audience*

# CHAPTER I

# The Church and Its Ministry

"Who is to assist whom in the ministry of the church?" asked Cameron P. Hall as he addressed religious leaders in a planning session. "Is the layman primarily to assist the clergy in the running and effective operation of the church or is it the primary function of the clergy to assist the laity in its ministry to the world?"

Georgia Harkness cites the results of one survey among twelve thousand laymen of one church body in which four options were presented, the respondent being asked to check the one most nearly stating his own view:

**Laymen are**
> members of the people of God called to a total ministry of witness and service in the world.
> those who are ministered to by the clergy who are the true church.
> people in part-time Christian service.
> nonordained Christians whose function is to help the clergy do the work of the church.

Of the 5,020 replies received, an overwhelming majority of 59.9 percent checked the fourth option. Apparently, laymen think of themselves chiefly as assistants to the ordained ministers.[1]

Is the church an institution with primary concerns for self-propagation and promotion or is it a fellowship through which the ministry of Christ himself is carried into the world? Are we substituting institutional promotion and statistical success for real evangelism, mission, and concern for people?

---

[1] *The Church and Its Laity* (New York and Nashville: Abingdon Press, 1962), pp. 15-16.

These are penetrating questions and are not intended to imply that the institutional phase of the church is something less than valid, but rather to put clearly into focus the difference between the means and the end, for we have tended to lose our way in "church work," neglecting or even forgetting what our real mission is.

The thesis of this book is that the whole church is a ministry —the ministry of Christ himself continued through his people, that every single Christian person must, in the very nature of the case, be a "minister," and that the group of full-time, paid servants of the church so commonly known as the "ministry" is really a ministry-within-the-ministry of the church as a whole.

This book is intended to offer some clues as to what the layman's ministry really is. It is intended to say something about the working relationships within the local congregation where people bear their individual and corporate witness.

At the outset there are certain fuzzy conceptions, even misconceptions, which ought to be clarified so that we may be thinking within the same context.

## Who Is a Minister?

There is, first of all, an erroneous conception of the term "ministry." To most people it means the *ordained* ministry. They think of the ministry as that group of religious leaders who are concerned with the running of the church, preaching sermons, promoting denominational or interdenominational work, counseling with people, administering the ordinances or sacraments, and often distinguished by a special garb that sets them apart from other people. They have a variety of titles and designations, depending upon the beliefs, customs, or ecclesiastical positions of their church bodies. They range from the itinerant preacher of the "Bible belt" to the colorfully garbed priests of an ecclesiastical hierarchy.

But, to minister means to serve. Indeed the word has a rather broad meaning. It may mean ministering to guests by serving food or administering of finance in government. In a specifically Christian way of thinking, however, ministry means the imparting of spiritual help under God. It suggests one who acts under the orders of God, who carries out God's orders and serves in his name. In this connection it has the sense of standing between another person and God and of serving God by serving one's fellowman. Jesus said, "Whosoever will be great among you, let him be your minister" (Matt. 20:26). He further insisted that he himself came for such purpose. "The Son of man came not to be ministered unto, but to minister, . . ." (vs. 28). To minister, then, in the Christian sense is to share with one's fellowman that which he has received from God. It is appropriate, therefore, to say "you have a ministry."

### ORDAINED MINISTER AND LAYMAN

Then there is often an artificial gap between the ordained minister and the layman, as though there were some basic difference in them as persons. There is no such basic distinction. The ordained man is as human, as subject to temptations and doubts as anybody else. He has no special corner on God, though presumably he has given more intensive thought and study to spiritual matters.

There is no basic difference between the call of God to live as a Christian when it comes to an ordained minister and that call when it comes to any other person. It is true that the ordained minister is called to a specialized work and to special preparation for that work. At the same time every Christian is called by God to Christian vocation and to making the service of God his primary purpose in life.

In the early days of the Christian church there was no clear or bold line of demarkation between the ordained ministry and the laity. It is true that the apostles and others called to similar capacity were, in a sense, set apart. This was because of their function and work, rather than because of a position in an ecclesiastical structure.

Perhaps the ordained ministry is less set apart in the public mind now than it was some years ago, but there is still the tendency to look upon the ministry as belonging to this special group known as the "clergy," whose primary business it is to run the church as an institution.

### THE CHURCH AS A FUNCTION

The conception of the church is so often a static one. Many people see the church primarily as an institution which is an end in itself or as people assembled together at a specific time and place. Is there not also a spiritual and dynamic concept of the church as *function* in daily life? We need to see the church as a whole.

The church must be seen not merely as people gathered together, but also as dispersed in the midst of life. The church's primary ministry is in the world. We come together to worship, to learn, to grow, and become better persons, but we go forth to bear our witness in our vocation, in our home, at play, as parent, as teacher, as neighbor, and friend. The church has an institutional aspect, but this is the *means,* not the end itself.

Some changes in rigid church structure may be needed in order to give this fact full expression, for the church must be conceived of in dynamic terms, in terms of *movement,* of *function,* of *ministry,* as the Christians who are called and who have learned and worshiped in the gathered assembly go forth to bear their witness in the manner for which they are best fitted.

In this book we shall see the church in terms of function, as the ministry of Christ continued through his people. We shall see it in human values, with one central question in focus: What real difference are we making in anybody's life or home?

### PHYSICAL AND SPIRITUAL

Some people make a false distinction between the physical and the spiritual, as though God were confined inside the walls of the church as an institution, and as though the only service to him must be something of a distinctly religious nature within the framework of a narrowly understood institution.

But God is the God of the world, too! He is the God of all of life. He is the God of commerce and trade, of agriculture, of growing things. He is the God of the marketplace, of science, of engineering, of mathematics, and even politics!

There is a very real sense in which any thing—organic or inorganic—if seen in depth will lead us to a sense of the universal and the eternal. Do you remember the words of Alfred Lord Tennyson?

> Flower in the crannied wall,
> I pluck you out of the crannies,
> I hold you here, root and all, in my hand,
> Little flower—but if I could understand
> What you are, root and all, and all in all,
> I should know what God and man is.

It is easy to get poetic about something so beautiful as a flower, but tell me, you carpenter, does "level" have any meaning at all for you beyond its mechanical implications? Does not a perfect circle or a perfect square speak of something beyond itself? Or tell me, you mathematician, does "two plus two equal four" say anything to you about universal laws? Do not the very figures you use in your calculations lead you ultimately to a sense of the infinite?

One thing Jesus did in the Incarnation was to wed the spiritual and the physical. He was no less the Son of God when he was standing amid the shavings of the carpenter shop than when he healed the sick. Can you not imagine his taking delight in a clean, smooth surface or a joint well fitted? And do you not, Mr. Layman, have a perfect right to find such joy in your toil, whatever it may be?

Romans 8 records a stout argument on the part of the Apostle Paul, about the carnal mind being an enemy of the spiritual mind. Some people take that to mean that the physical is forever at war with the spiritual, but, mind you, he was talking about the place of one's *thinking* and the *interpretation* one places upon life.

An old professor of mine was fond of saying that the spiritual man is one who draws from life a spiritual interpretation, who recognizes a stewardship in everything he is and everything he does.

### CHRIST IS CONTEMPORARY

There seems to be a common, though unexpressed, feeling that the work of Christ is something historical, which, if you believe it literally, will have magical qualities, and that there is some sort of virtue in the mere repetition of it. Take time to think that through!

The crucifixion, death, and resurrection of Christ are no mere historical events. They are *timeless!* They express eternal realities. They reveal God's own heart, his perpetual attitudes. They are forever contemporary. They are *here* and *now!*

Then, to follow Christ means to become involved. It is not the exercising of some magical power which throws all responsibility upon God and calls for his resources. It cannot be a substitute for action. We dare not separate "pray" from "work" or "think." Therefore, to be a Christian means to participate in the spirit and purpose and manner of the ministry which characterized our Lord. It is to throw one's self into God's unfinished work in the world. It is to be made his instrument in the answering of prayer. It is to enter into Christ's work, extending that work.

We have a book in the New Testament known as the Acts of the Apostles. Thank heaven it is not merely a book of resolutions of the apostles or even the devotional life of the apostles. These people became immediately involved in the work of the risen Lord, for his work was not yet completed. Paul wrote to the Colossians, "This is my way of helping to complete, in my poor human flesh, the full tale of Christ's afflictions still to be endured, for the sake of his body which is the church" (Col. 1:24, NEB).

Samuel Shoemaker once charged that the tragedy of so much religious activity is the fact that it consists simply in the professionals talking among themselves. Christian workers can become ingrown, very much concerned with internal affairs. Christianity began as a *powerful movement among laymen,* but it soon developed ideologies, rules, symbols, mores, folkways, habits, customs, creeds, peculiar types of behavior, and institutional patterns. There have been times in the history of the church when the institution was conceived not merely as the embodiment or expression of Christianity but as synonymous with it. These were times of weakness. We cannot deny the need for institutional forms, but we can "zero in" on the primary purpose for which the forms exist and indeed upon the essential nature of the church itself.

## Too Little Action

There is a legend about a playwright, cooped up in a telephone booth, holding the giant Manhattan telephone directory in his hands. He hefted its great bulk and looked curiously at its hundreds of pages of Cohens, Joneses, Smiths, O'Briens, and Johnsons. Thinking as a dramatist, he exclaimed, "There is not much of a plot here, but O boy, what a cast!"[2] Is that a parable? Church roles are heavily laden with the names of countless people who seldom or never attend a church service, much less get involved in any real ministry, either within the church or outside. What a cast! But where are the people? Where is the action?

You get quite a different picture in the New Testament, when to be a part of the church meant real involvement. The persecution was so heavy that only the most earnest and sin-

---

[2]Halford E. Luccock, *Marching Off the Map* (New York: Harper & Brothers, 1952), pp. 23.

cere dared make themselves a part of this dynamic movement. The Bible says, "And of the rest durst no man join himself to them: but the people magnified them" (Acts 5:13).

The New Testament church was on a battle line, not in a reservation or rest camp. And the whole body of believers seemed to be involved. They were followers of "the way," not members of an institution. They believed in one another. They loved one another. They worked together. There was a remarkable quality of fellowship and cooperation. Their concern was for saving *persons*.

Down across the years walls have been raised, and the insidious thing about walls is that they so easily become tombs. Put up to preserve life, they strangle it. Walls set up by the church to keep its gospel enclosed in the churchyard have become the tomb of a "dead" Christ. This entombed Christ, in the minds of his followers, does not count in the really important areas of life.

### BETWEEN THE CHURCH AND THE WORLD

Today there has developed a powerful movement, a kind of groundswell, among intelligent, dedicated, and resourceful laymen. And there is very great concern among many ordained ministers who look with heavy hearts upon the inactive, preoccupied laymen whose names are on their church rolls. If the imagination, genius, experience, and abilities of countless laymen could be brought in creative fashion to bear upon the church's life and work, and if the potential resources could be harnessed to witness for Christ in the midst of life, the tide of secularism and materialism might well be stemmed. Leisure time might be made creative, and a spiritual revival be realized.

There ought to be more interpenetration between the church and the world—the witness of Christ borne by intelligent laymen in the midst of life, and at the same time those laymen bringing to bear upon the church and its work the viewpoints, experience, and disciplines they have learned in their respective vocations. Church leaders will have to be willing to *listen* as well as to speak. It is doubtful that we can speak with much meaning unless we have also listened.

It is unthinkable that a dedicated Christian layman who is entrusted with responsibility in his business, profession, or industry would have only a passive and neutral role in the church. The viewpoints and know-how of many persons representing a wide range of interests and skills are necessary in helping to plan a total ministry to people of all walks of life and in bearing a combined witness in a complex, highly structured society. If we are to witness in all areas of life, our planning must arise from many viewpoints and from vastly more knowledge than any few persons possess. The ordained minister, while trained in his field, is not expert in all fields. If the work is left to him and a "faithful few," it will at last suffer for lack of virility, and the community will suffer because of its irrelevance to real needs.

In this book we shall have the local congregation pretty much in view. Mr. Layman, in your relation to the local church and in relation to your lifework, you have a ministry.

## For Discussion

1. In your own work, how do you see yourself related to the larger interests and needs of your fellowmen and to the kingdom of God?

2. How would you have answered to the four options on which laymen were asked to check their view of the layman's place?

3. What is your "image" of the minister, and how do you feel about the typical minister?

4. How do you feel about the church and your own relationship to it?

CHAPTER II

## *Person to Person*

If you go back to the very headwaters of your faith, you will find there not an organization nor a mere set of beliefs. You find a Person—Jesus Christ. He was talking about the Eternal Person and his love for every person. He was the Eternal Truth become a man. A Person leads us along the path of Christian faith.

Moreover, the individual person was always in the focus of his concern and attention. More important than rules and regulations was the person. He cut across the stratification of society to help the person. He even ignored the taboos in order to help a person. The person was more important in his eyes, for instance, than the law of the Sabbath, for as he said, "The Sabbath was made for man, not man for the Sabbath."

At the risk of overdoing a word, we can properly say that the gospel is the story of how the Eternal Person seeks persons through a Person. He could not stop with words, with laws or commandments or even a glorious history, or the challenging teaching of prophets. The Word had to become flesh in order to reach the hearts and minds of persons. And he was concerned not merely about mankind in general or people en masse. He was concerned with *each* individual person.

If we could reduce the ministry of Jesus in our understanding to its central purpose, what would it be? If one were to depict the gospel in the form of a target, what would be at the bull's eye? What is the central principle, the theme constantly reiterated? What is it that everything else expands, illustrates, and explains? What is the basic motif, the essential meaning

19

of it? Why did he perform miracles? One must conclude that it is love—first, last, and always.

Probably the Apostle John understood this better than any of the others. You can see him as an elderly man, writing to people he called his children, saying:

To us, the greatest demonstration of God's love for us has been his sending his only Son into the world to give us life through him. We see real love, not in the fact that we loved God, but that he loved us and sent his Son to make personal atonement for our sins. If God loved us as much as that, surely we, in our turn, should love one another! (1 John 4:9-11, Phillips).

The same apostle is translated by J. B. Phillips in John 3:16 as follows: "For God loved the world so much that he gave his only Son so that everyone who believes in him should not be lost, but should have eternal life." Familiar passages note that "He was moved with compassion on them," or "Jesus looking on him loved him." This is typical.

His temptations in the wilderness were the testing of the purity of his love. Tempted to use his power for personal ends, to make a display of himself, to succumb to the expectations of the crowd and thus gain favor and power, he refused them all and chose the way of lowly, humble service. Was this not the test of love's pure motive and purpose? He was the personification of love. He did not merely teach it. He actually lived it—utterly, completely, and without reserve. He gave himself and he made a test of our giving ourselves, too. This was the meaning of the cross. It is the meaning of your cross and mine.

Unfortunately, the word "love" has vague and uncertain meanings in our time. It ranges from cheap, sentimental meanings and even lust to the highest we know of self-giving and devotion. The English language here is not nearly so accurate or true as the original Greek, where different words were used to convey more accurate meanings. We are indebted to Dr. Anders Nygren for his scholarly treatment of this most important subject.

## DIVINE LOVE

While human love is stimulated, drawn forth or excited, divine love is unmotivated. That is, it is not drawn forth by the object of love, but rather arises out of the very nature of God himself. Says Dr. Nygren: "When it is said that God loves man, this is not a judgment on what man is like, but on what God is like."[1]

It is evident, then, that God's love does not depend upon one's worthiness. Jesus showed his love to publicans and sinners. He appeared to be more concerned about the worst elements in society than the nice people. His love was never controlled by its objects.

Closely allied in meaning here is the concept of indifference to value. While human love responds to manifest value, God's love creates value. Dr. Nygren offers this principle: "Any thought of valuation whatsoever is out of place in connection with fellowship with God. When God's love is directed to the sinner, then the position is clear; all thought of valuation is excluded in advance; for if God, the Holy One, loves the sinner, it cannot be because of his sin, but in spite of his sin."[2]

Human love is created. It is drawn forth. It is excited. But divine love creates. Dr. Nygren insists that divine love shares in the creativeness that is a mark of all the life of God. Agape is creative love. Divine love creates value in its objects.

Was not this true in the life of every person whom Jesus touched? That which was without value took on value. The person rejected by society, lost in rebellion and sin, becomes a new and different person, for as the Apostle John said, "As many as received him, to them gave he power to become the sons of God, even to them that believe on his name" (John 1:12).

Human love responds to fellowship. Divine love initiates

---

[1] *Agape and Eros* (Philadelphia: Westminster Press, 1953), pp. 75-76.
[2] *Ibid.*, pp. 77-78.

fellowship. It is a gift. When God meets man the initiative in establishing fellowship lies with divine love. To seek to enter into fellowship with God in any other way would be futile.

It can be seen, then, that human love is conditional. Divine love is unconditional. We must understand this because from this basic truth, all Christian love and Christian motivation must spring. If at any point this fundamental truth is neglected or overlooked, our Christian service will lack in depth and power.

### ANOTHER APPROACH

You might describe human love as a horizontal line, as re-action-in-kind. As human beings, we love those who are lovely. We are attracted to those who are attractive.

But divine love must be described more like a vertical line, the line of revelation. Jesus Christ revealed the nature of God. He also revealed the true nature of man. He was called the Son of God. He was also called the Son of Man.

He set down upon the horizontal line of man's reaction to man a totally new concept, that of God's love, and of the image of God in every person. Jesus seemed to look deep into each person's heart and life, to see the image of God there, the spark of divine life, and by his faith and love to set the whole personality aflame. Jesus did not *react* to that which was superficial in man as others did. Rather he *acted upon the essential nature of man and recreated him.* He was not defeated by appearance or by surface conduct. He saw deeper. He did not merely gravitate to people who were attractive. He gravitated to people who needed him, for his purpose was one of redemption, not pleasure.

The Apostle John may be quoted again, "We see real love, not in the fact that we loved God, but that he loved us" (1 John 4:10, Phillips). The religion of Jesus Christ, therefore, is not man's upreach, or his achievement, or his altruism. It lies, rather, in God's downreach, the overwhelming of man by divine love. The Apostle Paul, in exultant praise, cries, "Thanks be unto God for his unspeakable gift" (2 Cor. 9:15).

If you will turn to the Sermon on the Mount (Matt. 5–7) you will hear Jesus saying again and again, "Ye have heard that it hath been said . . . but I say unto you, . . ." (5:38).

Instead of following the old pattern of reaction-in-kind, he demands a new and higher standard of conduct—love your enemies, pray for those who are spiteful to you, turn the other cheek, break through this vicious circle of reaction-in-kind which snowballs into major conflict. Seize the initiative by the power of love. This was Jesus' new standard, a higher plane of living.

So Jesus, taking his place among men, lifted the horizontal line up upon the vertical one and made himself a cross. His conflict with entrenched power came because he loved and lifted people. He not only taught that men were free. He acted on that premise. His life was at cross angles with the practice of his time, and the cross is the symbol of that antithesis. His was a doctrine fought by the priests, for it took away their prerogatives and stripped them of their coercive powers. The teaching of Jesus offered men the maximum opportunity for growth, development, and freedom. He had an unfailing and unerring clue for justice in every situation. It was that love is the only real justice. It is the only climate in which a person can breathe free as a person.

## THE NATURE OF CHRISTIAN LOVE

Is this same thing demanded of the Christian? Is this a practicable standard which Jesus set? Who has not had the feeling of utter futility upon reading the teaching of Jesus to love our enemies and pray for those who despitefully use us. How can a man find it within himself to obey this from the heart?

Christian love has its prototype and ground in divine love as seen in Jesus Christ. It begins in surrendering to God's love, humbly accepting his unspeakable gift. In absolute unworthiness we have been taken in, loved, forgiven, redeemed. So we are, first of all, the *objects* of his love. Next, we must become, also, the *channels* of his love.

But we must see that this love is *not a mere ethical quality which we cultivate, but a divine quality to which we yield.* You cannot generate this love. You cannot produce it yourself. You can only yield to it and, in yielding, become the channel for it. Martin Luther insisted that we are the channels of "downpouring, outpouring love."

Jesus commanded us to love—to love God with all our hearts, souls, minds, and strength, and to love our neighbors as ourselves. But how does one do this? Do you blow on your hands and try hard? Do you grit your teeth and say, "I'll love if it kills me"? This we cannot continually do. Let us once again be instructed by the Apostle John:

> God is love, and the man whose life is lived in love does, in fact, live in God, and God does, in fact, live in him. So our love for him grows more and more, filling us with complete confidence for the day when he shall judge all men—for we realize that our life in this world is actually his life lived in us (1 John 4:16, Phillips).

If we are ever to live as Jesus commanded us to live, we must have the *viewpoint* of Jesus and the *spirit* of Jesus. We must yield completely to the spirit which controlled him. We must remember that love in the sense we are discussing it here is not primarily a human emotion or a feeling. It is more like a viewpoint, a creative insight, a redemptive faith. It is not merely an emotional reaction to another person, then, but a redemptive attitude under God. It is remembering God's own love and mercy to us and extending that mercy to others in his name and by his power.

The love of God is thus mediated through human hearts and minds, reaching out in redemptive witness, not in pride but in humble thanks.

"Evangelism," says D. T. Niles "is one beggar telling another where to find bread." The best witness is just that—a witness, not an argument or a judgment, but a witness. It is to say "this Christ has done for me," that by the witness one may inspire the faith of another with similar needs.

To have God's love means the same as to be possessed by him. If we have God himself, then we have nothing more to gain, for he is our all. One can, then, love with pure and holy devotion. Such love is unfeigned, and without pretense.

## FRUIT OF THE SPIRIT

Love is mentioned by Paul as the first of the fruits of the spirit, in Galatians 5:22. Jesus explained that love is the fulfillment of the law, the principle upon which all the laws and commandments are based. He insisted that this would be the test by which people around us would know that we belong to him, that we love one another.

In the Apostle Paul's first letter to the Corinthians, there is one short chapter which remains as perhaps the greatest gem of all the apostles' writings. Well-known to thousands upon thousands of people is 1 Corinthians 13. Read it carefully and you will see that what Paul is saying here is the very crux and heart of all Christian teaching—love for one's fellowman, love that does not seek to control or possess, love that finds no rejoicing in another's inferiority or failure, love that does not look with impatience upon one's fellowman to condemn and destroy, but love that looks with divine insight and patience, "believing all things, enduring all things."

We are called to follow Christ, who by his spirit, his teaching, and his love, removed barriers between man and God and between man and man, who set people right with God and with one another, who taught us to forgive that we may be forgiven, and to never go through the pretense of worship while there was some barrier between us and our brother.

## OUR CONCERN IS PERSONS

As Jesus' concern was persons, so must our concern be persons. The business of the church is not statistical success or institutional promotion. Those are only means to the end. Our real ministry must be measured in terms of love for persons and service to them. Without this as our primary motive, our many activities get out of hand and we lose perspective, forgetting what Christianity is really all about.

Christ became our servant in order that we might become servants. As he came not to be ministered unto but to minister, so must we. As he knelt humbly to wash the feet of his followers, so we must kneel in humble service to God by serving our fellowman.

My own work happens to be that of administration in the work of the church. It involves work behind a desk and behind a pulpit. But traveling across the length and breadth of the country, as well as moving among my neighbors and friends, I have tried to find opportunity for a person-to-person ministry. Such opportunities and experiences linger in my heart like a long-loved melody. It is the most real thing that I do, and I have the distinct feeling that if I fail in that personal ministry, then whatever I do behind a desk or behind the pulpit is something less than valid. I do not ask that the institutional work of the church be discontinued, but let us not forget *why* we do all these things.

At the headwaters of our faith there is a Person. Misunderstanding and confusion is shorn away as we go to him in imagination and faith, and try to follow in his footsteps, imbibe of his spirit, and yield ourselves as channels of his love.

You have a ministry. It is His ministry continued through you. As he ministered in the midst of life wherever he found persons, so we must find opportunity to express his love in natural and real ways. This is the real ministry of Christ. The primary business of the church is a ministry in the world through individuals like you and me, each in his own place, each in his own way, each in his own "world."

Now let us turn for a moment and look at the "world" in which one's ministry must take place.

### For Discussion

1. How have you been thinking of love? What has it meant to you?

2. Do you think it is possible to love one's neighbor as Jesus commanded?

3. What relation is there between Christian love and one's emotions?

4. Do you find it difficult to be deeply concerned about another person, except one of your own family or a close friend?

5. What changes must take place in us before we can be channels of God's love?

*Your real world is the setting
of your vocation, friendships,
thought, and feeling.*

# CHAPTER III

# Your "World"

It is interesting to note the casual way in which the prophet Amos is introduced: "The words of Amos, who was among the shepherds of Tekoa, which he saw concerning Israel in the days of Uzziah king of Judah . . ." (Amos 1:1, RSV). He was "one of the boys," a layman responsive to the divine Spirit. He was a working man, one who labored, looked, listened—and finally spoke.

The remarkable thing was that when Amos spoke, people listened and remembered. He was first dated by the fact that he spoke "two years before the earthquake." Later people seemed to forget the earthquake and remember his message. Now we know of the earthquake only because of its mention in connection with his earthshaking words. He was in a sense a layman, attuned to God and keenly observant of national needs.

Today we have countless laymen who are relatively unknown. But God can speak to and through them as he did through Amos. Consecrated laymen today can do things more memorable than an earthquake. Dr. Elton Trueblood says:

It is the recorded experience of various communities that the . . . evangelism of laymen and women is peculiarly effective, whereas a pastor's call on the same people may have had little or no influence. The chief reason for this difference seems to be the deep feeling that the pastor is only doing his required or routine work, whereas the layman's call is a happy surprise. The pastor is supposed to be for the church, much as the labor organizer is for the union, but the lay worker who makes a call is credited with calling out of genuine conviction, concern or even friendship.[1]

---

[1]*Your Other Vocation* (New York: Harper & Brothers, 1952), p. 41.

Does this mean that the word and witness of a layman is actually more effective than that of a clergyman? In many situations and for many people, the answer is Yes. As a New York waiter was heard to say, "There is no reason why a man can't serve roast beef and God at the same time."

## WHERE IS THE "WORLD"?

We are all in agreement that the mission of the church is "into all the world." What does this mean? We commonly think of the geographical world, especially other countries where the gospel has never been preached. This, of course, is always a mandate before us. There are vast areas and millions of people yet relatively untouched, and the task yet remaining is very great. We are now giving much thought to new approaches and methods whereby the Christian witness can be given by laymen who go to other lands in some "secular" capacity. Someone has spoken of Christian "guerrillas" to describe this kind of approach.

But a geographical conception alone is not enough. There are areas of life and experience as well. People may live on the same street and yet live in quite separate "worlds." Or even in the same house! Sometimes our communication is almost nil. We go our separate ways knowing little or nothing about a next-door neighbor, what he thinks or how he feels. The man who goes to church and perhaps serves in some official position may live in the same neighborhood with another whose world of living is the opposite of his.

There is the world of vocation. A person's work takes him into certain circles and relationships each working day. Here is where he feels the pressures, engages in the conflicts, senses the rewards of approval, suffers under unfavorable comparison, and, in a very real sense, lives his life. His wife at home lives in a different world, his children at school in another, his neighbor in another, and the city councilman in another.

There is the world of business, of trade, of finance, of government, of agriculture, of pedagogy. There is the world of capital and of labor, of race and color, of privilege and poverty.

Even a person's body is a part of his world. In a time of sickness or handicap, the most important thing in the world may be whether or not he can wiggle his toe or stand upright or walk. And how he compares with others in physical appearance may loom very large on his horizon.

To go into all the world we must concern ourselves with the stratification of society, the cleavages among men, the sufferings of minority groups, and many other aspects of the world. We must be aware of each man's world. The gospel goes into *life*, not into geographical districts. It is not primarily concerned with places but with *persons*. When Jesus gave to his followers the Great Commission, he certainly had people in mind. He always did.

### FROM THE INSIDE

During World War II, saboteurs played a tremendously destructive role. They had influence grossly out of proportion to their numbers. The "fifth column" is now almost forgotten language, but the power of inside workings cannot be discounted. This applies in Christian witness, too. Far more effective than an outside frontal attack is the inside influence. The word of a knowledgeable person at the right time and place—and in the right manner—is strategic. The boy David slew the giant Goliath with a slingshot and a pebble *well placed,* at a vulnerable spot.

Far more important, for instance, than propaganda from Russia is the quality of our own people living and working in America. Who can underestimate the power of good citizenship? It is said that the National Municipal League in New York City outlines seven ills of government: popular apathy and ignorance, undemocratic methods in elections, spoils and corruption, wasteful and antiquated systems, overlapping services, hand-to-mouth planning and financing, and unnecessary centralization and bureaucracy. Do you know what they figured out as the remedy? The League gives it in four words: "Active and informed citizens."[2]

*Information Service* stated, "Only when it is challenged does the case for Christian behavior develop in all its strength and power . . . Religion is forced into a false position if it is confined behind the doors of the religious broadcasting department. Both the manner and the content of Christian apologetic will change for the better when religion speaks again, not only through the voice of the clerics in their unanswerable pulpits, but through the voices of men in science, artists and laymen of all kinds, for whom religion is . . . always indirectly mediated through their life's work and through the language which that work teaches them to speak."[3]

But laymen must speak! Too many of them have the policy of the stupid monkey trio, with the inane motto, "Speak no evil, see no evil, hear no evil," and they cling to that triple inactivity as a high expression of the conduct of a Christian, if not a summary of the gospel itself. But in the face of sin, of injustice, of wrong, of error, the true Christian has a commission to something other than to be dumb, blind, and deaf. He is to proclaim right versus wrong. He must search and separate good from evil. He must keep his senses alert and know the truth. He must be, if necessary, a revolutionist against the status quo. We have had Pollyannas and Milquetoasts galore, but the world moves forward on the feet of people who have convictions. A superior and contented smile may be simply stupid. Silence is not always golden. Sometimes it is just plain yellow! You can't very well be bodily in the world but spiritually outside it.

"If Christians are to be effective in public affairs," said John Foster Dulles, "they must not be mere spectators. They must be actors in an arena where it may be necessary to seek and accept

---

[2]*Cappers Weekly*, January 8, 1950.
[3]Issue of September 7, 1946.

provisionally what is less than Christian perfection."[4] It is sad that many people do not take their religion with them into their places of business, for fear of losing it.

## THE CHURCH AND THE WORLD

When Jesus prayed for his disciples, as recorded in John 17, commonly known as the high-priestly prayer, he beseeched the Father as follows: "I do not pray that thou shouldst take them out of the world, but that thou shouldst keep them from the evil one. They are not of the world, even as I am not of the world. . . . As thou didst send me into the world, so I have sent them into the world" (John 17:15-16, 18, RSV). In the world, but not of it, yet sent into it! The question is *how?*

How is the church to go into the world? As an institution? As a force in politics? As an arbiter in labor-management relations? Some people think so. They claim the church is "behind the times." I insist that its work lies "behind the scenes." Its message is what the ages have to say to the passing hours.

Sir Stafford Cripps, British Chancellor of the Exchequer, once advised the Church of England to stay out of coming British elections. Said he, "We do not want politics in our religion, but we do want Christian standards in our politics."[5]

The church as an institution is not involved in the world of business, of commerce, trade, agriculture, or politics. Its business is to *prepare persons* to bear a Christian witness and to express Christian standards in the midst of varied vocations. By this means and this alone can the church insinuate the Christian message into every man's world. The ordained minister is not to be criticized because he is not personally involved in the problems that beset each businessman or each man of another profession than his own. The church is not to be criticized because it is not directly involved in what some people call the "real world."

———
[4]*Quote,* November 23, 1952.
[5]*Quote,* November 27, 1949.

Even though a business may spread itself over the whole world and may employ 100,000 men, the average person will usually form his judgment of that business through his contact with one individual, and, so it is with the church. If that one contact is rude or inefficient, it will take a lot of kindness and efficiency on the part of many others to overcome a bad impression. The church goes into every area of life, as *you* go into *your* area of life. Every man bears his witness in his own "world."

## WHAT IS YOUR WORLD?

Your world is your vocation, the framework of your life. Through it you bear your witness in the midst of life. Your vocation will pretty well determine the economic scale upon which you live. It will very strongly influence your circle of friends. It will bring you in contact intimately with some social and economic issues. It is your *principal involvement* in life.

Real witness in the world today happens through intelligent, knowledgeable, dedicated laymen, as they bear their witness outside the church apparatus and outside the specific times, places, and types of activity known as "church work." The real Christian witness is expressed through your attitude, your spirit, your scale of values, your interrelationship with persons.

The church penetrates into society through you, and all the influence and status you have earned by your skill and dedicated labor will have a great bearing upon your Christian witness.

It is interesting to note that it has not been armies or navies that have advanced the human race, but here and there, in the course of the ages, an individual who has stood up and cast his shadow with courage and daring. It has not appeared so at the time or in the eyes of the man himself, but what he did and what he stood for went on and on.

A man may not be able to see very far by the light of his candle, but his candle itself can be seen from a long way off. During World War II we had the blackouts. Dark blinds were to be drawn over every window, being careful that no cracks let the light shine through. We were told that a ray of light, even a small one, could be seen at a great distance. Many laymen don't realize the strength of their own witness.

Your own age group is an area of influence. Young people have influence with young people. Women have their own unique influence with other women. Certainly men have influence with men. Undoubtedly a man has a special kind of influence in his home and family. Your influence is a responsibility under God. You can capitalize on such natural associations in age groups and neighborhood circles.

Your special interests or hobbies may hold a clue for you. And very probably the greater your skill the more influence you will have. Many a man has been influenced for Christ on the golf course. There is something about fishing that seems to open a fellow's heart, and the long evenings at a hunting lodge may bring opportunities unheard of at any other time. Such times as these may be golden opportunities for you to perform the kind of personal ministry which would change someone's life and bring you lifelong rewards in satisfaction.

Many a wife and mother has said to me, "If only you could spend more time with my son [or my husband]." But an ordained minister has only so much time, and actually he will have less influence with many sons and husbands than would the layman. A Christian witness can be borne in countless places, in countless ways, by countless methods. What it takes is the spirit, the mindfulness, the alertness to do it.

It is as Christ gets into the warp and woof of our living, therefore, that he finds witness in the world. This must come through a church which has spread throughout the world. It has penetrated Western civilization, affecting its standards and its sense of values. It did so not primarily as an institution but as a ministry which found its way through the witness of intelligent laymen in business and professions, in government, and in the marketplace.

Our real hope is grounded on the fact that in a thousand

and one ordinary daily experiences, good will work and win out. Friendship is effective. Love is contagious. The witness of Christ will not die. What you do is a leaven in the lump. The lump is very large, it is true, but many bits of leaven at work could change the course of history. The most powerful instrument you have is example. The best way to prove a stick is crooked is to lay a straight one beside it.

And as Calvin Coolidge once said, "We cannot do everything at once, but we can do something at once."

## THE WORLD OF YOUR EXPERIENCE

Your world is the world of your thought life, your sense of failure, your confidence in the skills you possess, the guilt you carry in your heart. The most real world you live in often is this world of your own experience. It can be a millstone around your neck or it can be your means of service.

It will be a millstone if you live in regret, mulling over your mistakes again and again, breaking your own heart. Such an attitude will keep you living in turmoil and tension continually. You can condemn yourself, you can wallow in regret, you can feel sorry for yourself, and blame other people. But regret is wasted time. You cannot build a thing on regret. You can only wallow in it, and that is about all. It will poison what is left of life, and you will be much less able to meet the future.

Or, on the other hand, you can live in the past with pride and say, "Things are not like they used to be," or "Oh, for the good old days." There are a great many people who cancel themselves out of present-day living and render themselves negligible as personalities because of this tendency to hail back to another day. By this means, also, your experience can be like a millstone around your neck.

Your experience, on the other hand, can be your raw material for the future. You can draw from its resources. You can allow yourself to be taught. You can project into the future and achieve new usefulness, turning even your bitterest experiences into a blessing.

Your imagination uses experience as its raw material. You cannot project into areas where you are totally without experience, but your experience can be set into new combinations and new relationships by the use of imagination. This often holds the real key to the best ministry you can perform to others.

A certain teacher of young preachers advised them to get as many different kinds of experience as possible before entering the ministry—in the factory, on the farm, in the shop, among people of all kinds, in this country and abroad. He suggested that one might get a job on a boat and work his way around the world. Why did he give this advice? Because, he said, the more different kinds of experience he has, the more he can understand other people and minister to them. How else can one minister except out of his experience?

There is an unforgettable experience, when as a young pastor I called upon a middle-aged lady whose husband had passed away an hour or so before. I attempted to read the right Bible verses and to say the right things, and to give the right advice, as I had been taught. But she laid her hand on my arm, stopping me, and said, "I know you mean well and I appreciate your effort, but you don't really know what you are talking about." She said it with respect, and she was right. I had only words to offer—ideas. But in that moment I made my decision to stop next at the home of a lady who had been widowed a year or so before. I asked her to take my place by that woman's side, and to minister to her out of her own experience. She did. The result was wonderful!

If you had a deep need, to whom would you turn? To someone with only finespun theories? To someone with only philosophical answers? Hardly. You would turn to one who had had a similar experience and who could say to you, "This is the way I found it." So even *your* experience can be a blessing.

Abraham Lincoln was a success, held in high honor in the annals of history. He is remembered for his great humanitarianism, his understanding heart, his charity for all. But what made him great? It was his experience in which a great mind and imagination was at work. He was born and reared in poverty, so he knew the meaning of toil. He had the pain of knowing grave uncertainties in his parental home. He knew the heartaches and embarrassment of severe tension in his own home. He suffered the loss of dearly loved sons (and who could better write a letter of consolation to a mother who had lost her own sons in the fratricidal Civil War?). His service to the nation and to his suffering brothers of the human race arose directly from a heart disciplined and taught by sorrow and pain. Experience equipped him and we love him.

### You Are Priest

The word "priest" immediately conjures up images of someone in ecclesiastical garb, performing certain ritualistic ceremonies, but in a sense, every person is a priest. It means one who performs a sacrificial, interpretative or ministerial function. It is one who serves or ministers. It need not refer only to the official and ordained ministry of the church, but to every single Christian who ministers.

Right here is the nub of our problem in the church. Ministry and service are seen as something belonging to a special professional class, when in New Testament terms every Christian is a minister. Every Christian is a priest in the sense that he stands between some other person and God, and performs a ministry of mediation. He conveys God's message. We serve one another in Christ's name. Jesus Christ is the ultimate priest, minister, and servant, but the whole church is priestly and ministerial. Each person is, in a sense, responsible for his neighbor. "We are all priests," wrote Luther, "insofar as we are Christians."

Ministry in this sense is closer to the common life. It reaches people where they are. It is simple, direct, related to life in meaningful ways.

The man on the street has little understanding of religion, and much of the vocabulary is strange to him. Much of our time in the church seems to be taken up answering questions that he is not asking. His image of the church is a very professional one, very institutional, and quite removed from life. But when he meets a vital Christian, whose life touches his in a meaningful way, he will listen, for this is language he understands.

This is the business of the layman who is in the midst of life far more than the ordained minister can be. If the layman can be an effective witness, beginning with a man's own frame of thinking, using language he understands, sharing out of experience and supporting his words by a godly life, the effect cannot help but be deep and lasting. As Elton Trueblood has said:

> Most words of a clergyman are minimized simply because he is supposed to say them. A pastor's convictions are discounted because he is supposed to have a professional stake in the effort to make them prevail. Sometimes people sink so low as to remark that this is what he is paid for; he is on the side of the angels by virtue of his employment. The contrast in effect is often enormous when a layman's remarks are taken seriously, even though he says practically the same words. His words are given full weight, not because he is a more able exponent, but because he is wholly free from any stigma of professionalism.[6]

Your witness, therefore, will arise out of personal friendship and confidence. It will be enhanced by your success or skill. It will be given depth by your own experience, even your experience of failure, for you will not take your place as some superior person who has "arrived," but as a human being, with his feet on the earth as much as anybody else—as one who stands bareheaded under God, having experienced forgiveness and grace.

What, then, is your ministry? Only you can tell. And you will know only as it unfolds to you. Perhaps these words of Toyohiko Kagawa will have some meaning for you:

> I cannot invent
> New things,
> Like the airships
> Which sail

[6]Trueblood, *op. cit.*, pp. 40-41.

On silver wings;
But today
A wonderful thought
In the dawn was given,
And the stripes on my robe,
Shining from wear,
Were suddenly fair,
Bright with a light
Falling from Heaven—
Gold, and silver, and bronze
Lights from the windows of Heaven.

And the thought
Was this:
That a secret plan
Is hid in my hand;
That my hand is big,
Big,
Because of this plan.

That God,
Who dwells in my hand,
Knows the secret plan
Of the things He will do for the world
Using my hand![7]
                    —Toyohiko Kagawa

## For Discussion

1. How would you describe your own "world"? In your discussion group, try to understand one another's "worlds" of vocation, thought, feeling, home.
2. To whom do you turn for counsel or understanding? What are the factors that determine whose counsel you seek?
3. Have you been able to use your experience as a ministry to someone else? How often? In what ways?
4. Do you see ways in which you can minister in your "world" to people where they really live?

---

[7]*Songs of the Slums* (Nashville: Cokesbury Press, 1935), pp. 66-67.

*"They could not see
the bitter smile
behind the painted
grin he wore."*

# CHAPTER IV

## The Person Behind the Face

An eminent teacher and preacher of America related a story told him by a friend who was a missionary in China. It seems the missionary was "called into a textile mill in China, to identify a child worker, just eleven years of age, who had fallen asleep at a machine, and been mangled to death. He said that as he looked at the pitiful body, he realized that the whole affair was a profoundly theological question: What is she? Just one of the four hundred million *things* in China, things which were very useful in producing a 200 percent profit?"[1] The lesson drawn from this story was that what we are willing to do for men depends ultimately on our conception of what they actually are. If we put on them the rating of immortal souls, that act of faith brings a new and powerful momentum into action on their behalf. When we carry that estimate of men into our action, Jesus really does get loose in the world, as an overturning and saving force.

To the Greek in Jesus' day every foreigner was a barbarian. To the Jew every stranger was a Gentile dog. To every Mohammedan, every alien was an infidel. Jesus came and erased every condemning title from the dictionaries of mankind and wrote there the word "brother." Every human being is a brother to every other human being, and Christians, of all people, ought to know that, to think it and feel it.

### EACH MAN IN HIS WORLD

You see a man on the street. He looks confident, even jaunty. But follow him home. Sit down with him by the fire and look

---

[1]Luccock, *op. cit.*, p. 87.

41

into his heart. Measure his thoughts. Plumb his feelings. You may find that he is a different man from the one you saw on the street, for the compensations and defenses he has erected and the role he plays might be very misleading.

See the busy executive behind his desk. Secretaries and office boys come and go. Reports are laid before him. Instructions are given. He barks orders and people listen. He is important. He is the picture of confidence. But sit beside his bed as he lies down to rest. Feel the relationships of his home. Share the dark fears of financial failure, or the guilt of an infidelity, or the concern over a wayward son, or perhaps a marriage long neglected and now near the breaking point. Here is where he really lives. This is his *world*.

A man can be torn apart by conflicting loyalties. He may be a lawyer with heavy professional responsibilities. He may be trying to save a home, and with a feeling of guilt that he should do much more, but is prevented. He is a member of a service club, chairman of a finance drive, a baseball fan, a church member, a husband, a father—with not enough time or strength for all these various roles. His wife may be a spendthrift, living beyond their means. He is pressured to live in the biggest house in the neighborhood, and in the best neighborhood. There is pressure from every direction to buy more, to do more, to work harder, to try harder.

But what about the man as a person? What about the person behind the face? If you are ever to minister it must be to this person behind the face. You must be willing to move from your own world of preoccupations and go to another man's world, there to see through his eyes, to understand what is in his heart. You must think and feel yourself into another man's flesh and life, so to speak. People are well-nigh dying for the need of this kind of ministry.

Visiting a woman in the hospital, I was instructed not to disclose to her the fact that she had cancer. She was about ready for surgery. One simple question brought a flood of tears. "Are you afraid?" I asked, and she answered, "I have never been so scared in my life. I feel so alone. I know the doctor is telling the members of my family more than he tells me." Then I asked her, "What do you think is wrong with you?" She answered, "Don't tell my family, but I think I have cancer." I was true to my promise and I did not confirm her fear, but my heart was heavy that this suffering soul was so alone, so removed from understanding and real communication. She talked out her fear and went to surgery with more confidence, now that someone understood.

Probably every person puts up some sort of front and, to a certain degree, wears a mask. A mask is very deceptive. You don't help a person much by reacting to the mask. Christian love calls for an understanding of the person behind the face.

### Battered by the World Outside

With our present-day massification of human society and the impersonal nature of many of our relationships, there comes a deep loneliness. One may live in a large city amid thousands of people and yet lack a personal relatedness to any one of them. He can stand in the middle of Times Square and be utterly alone. David Riesman has written of "the lonely crowd"— this depersonalized human society where there is so much of estrangement, alienation, and lostness, and the threatening forces over which he has no control.[2]

This loneliness is terrible, because one finds little of the basic satisfactions in life. He conforms because that is the thing to do. He may wear the latest style in clothes, drive a late-model car, and live in a good neighborhood. He fits in with the organization like a cog in a machine, but often his most basic needs are denied.

Any direction he looks his mind is battered by advertising, calling for new loyalties or commitments. He must buy this or do that in order to keep up with the neighbors. New tastes and desires are created. He is pressured into living beyond his

---

[2]*The Lonely Crowd*, (New York: Doubleday, 1953).

means. He lives in the thick of thin things. Entertainment is often geared to his baser impulses. Noise batters his eardrums. Time limits make him curse every stoplight, and he feels guilty because he cannot do more.

But a person has basic needs beyond food, clothing, and things. He needs recognition as a person. He needs love, understanding, and communication with other persons as persons. We ought to remember the words of that great Harvard psychologist, William James, when he said, "The deepest principle of human nature is the craving to be appreciated."

At the airport I saw a gasoline truck pull up to refuel an airplane. First, they clamped a copper cable from the plane to the truck. Why? Gasoline trucks used to explode when the nozzle would touch the metal of the plane because of static electricity. Now they hang a chain from the truck to the pavement so it touches. Did you ever slide your feet over a rug, then touch somebody and see a spark fly? Something like this happens in people. Tensions build up so they are ready to explode. Connection eases the tension. Understanding lets off the pressure.

Why do people waste their lives with the use of alcohol, sexual excesses, and pleasure-madness? In many cases it is sheer escape. It is about the only release they know. Customarily, then, Christians stand around to cluck their tongues and say, "Shame, shame," but make very little effort to understand the *person*. The kind of Christian teaching that speaks only to man's outer conduct is a poor substitute for the teaching of Jesus and an even poorer substitute for his love.

## YOUR ENEMY

If you get a dog in a corner, he is likely to snarl and even bite. People also snarl when they get in corners. But the man looking on doesn't recognize the corners, for they are emotional.

Jesus taught us to love our enemies, to pray for those who despitefully use us. Does this mean we are to make a pretense

of this and mouth a prayer out of a sense of duty, or in Pharisaical fashion to utter these prayers in the company of other
people, to impress them with our righteousness?

It would seem that Jesus beckoned us beyond the world of
appearance—and judging by the snarl—to a deeper understanding of the person and the *reason* for the snarl. When he prayed
for his crucifiers on the cross, the last part of his recorded
words are significant: "Father, forgive them, *for they know not
what they do.*" He was not willing to conclude that they were
as evil as they appeared to be. He was not judging their appearance, but understanding, in some way, their warped scale
of values and the pressures that were brought to bear upon
them. This is love—to understand the person behind the face.

Psychologists tell us that often people hate themselves. Joshua
L. Liebman said, "We know that our mental hospitals are
filled with extremists who mutilate themselves physically. But
all the streets of the world are teeming with men and women
who mutilate themselves spiritually and mentally in the invis-
ible ways of self-criticism and self-degradation."[3] Cruelties to
others arise out of twisted, warped emotions; irrational action
is the result. "Sadism," he says, "certainly does not tell the
whole story about man; it merely indicates that men and women
destroy and hate out of a feeling of their own hopelessness
and frustration, out of a desire to take vengeance upon the
world for their own inner distortions and emotional conflicts.
Again and again it is being demonstrated in psychological
clinics that when these distortions and conflicts are resolved,
the basic trend in human nature toward love and the affirmation
of other personalities manifests itself."[4]

Is Jesus' teaching, then, just so much idealism? No, it is the
starkest realism! The only real redemption. But he needs followers who can see behind the face. Let me quote Dr. Liebman
again: "Love and hate are emotions which attach themselves

---

[3]*Peace of Mind* (New York: Simon & Schuster, 1946), p. 41.
[4]*Ibid.*, p. 73.

at times to other persons and at times to ourselves. It is one of the great discoveries of modern psychology that our attitudes toward ourselves are just as complicated as our attitude to others—sometimes more so. The great commandment of religion, 'Thou shalt love thy neighbor as thyself,' might now be better interpreted to mean, 'Thou shalt love thyself properly, and *then* thou wilt love thy neighbor.' "[5]

Jesus Christ identified himself with the needs of men and women everywhere and for all time. To follow him truly is to follow him in such love. And the successful issue of the appeal for harmony in the world is to be found in spiritual expansion, the understanding of other persons, in love.

Someone has spoken of an "audacious offensive" in the name of Christ. Jesus did not teach passive resistance, but an *active* resistance on a higher level. The account does not say, "If a man smite you on the one cheek, let him smite the other also," but it does say, "Turn to him the other also." It is this offensive of love that forces the offender to go further and thus to break down. He tries to violate your proper rights. You, as a Christian, try to reach his heart. In turning the other cheek you take the offensive from him and seize the moral initiative in the situation. You set your own battleground, and choose your own weapons. You compel him to stand on ground with which he is not familiar and to face weapons he is not accustomed to facing. If a man forces you to go with him one mile, you are his slave; but if you voluntarily go with him two miles, you rise from your slavery, and become the victor. If he sues you at law and takes away your coat, you are his victim, but if you, without litigation, give him your overcoat also, you assume the mastery by moral courage.

## WHO CARES FOR ME?

Let us go, in imagination, and sit down with the person behind the face, the person who is barraged by every conceivable appeal, and hear him say, "Who really cares for me as a person? Everybody wants me to buy something or join something or support something. Everybody wants to use me or to count me as one of his members, but who cares for me as a person?"

Walk with this person behind the face as he goes down the street and sees the tall church edifice. What is going on in his mind? Listen in: What happens inside those gray walls and beneath that steeple? What kind of people go there? Just the well-to-do, the respectable? What kind of person is the pastor? Somebody with pious pronouncements, who is seen on special occasions in a special kind of role and who has a great zeal to get a large congregation and be important in the eyes of men? If I went inside, they would want me to join, but why would they want me to join? So they could count my nose next Sunday and get my contribution? Would they care, really, anything about *me?* Would I really be accepted in their group? *Would these be his thoughts?*

To what extent do we of the church give people the impression that they are just "church timber"? As a matter of fact, to what extent do we think of it that way and act that way? Just why do we want people to come to the church? Dare we examine our own motives and cut through our rationalizations with merciless honesty? Would we dare to admit that the man on the street sometimes senses a little *too much* our real motives?

No one knows better than the pastor the importance of maintaining and even promoting the church in its organized work. But what, in heaven's name, is the message we are conveying to the man on the street outside the church building? Where and in what manner are we saying to him, "God really loves you and we really love you." Are our moralizations and our preachments enough? Is it sufficient to speak to his external problems? What about the person behind the face, behind the habit patterns, the appearance, the sin?

We will reach this person only as some individual reaches

him through his own interests, in terms that he understands. The message of Jesus Christ is not conveyed by preaching alone, important as that is. It is conveyed as life touches life. This is the real ministry.

## SOMEBODY WITH A FACE

Have you heard the little story of the boy who is being put to bed by his mother? He was afraid of the dark and she was trying to console him, saying, "God is with you." And the little fellow protested, "But I want somebody with a face." It is not enough to tell people, "God loves you." They need somebody with a face.

God sent Jesus so that love would have a face, so that truth would be expressed in a human being—the Word become flesh. The difficulty, as someone has expressed it, is that the Word becomes words. We preach and pass resolutions. We are long on words. It is only when the Word becomes flesh that people understand and get the message.

One summer evening I sat in my car with a young man beside me. A streetlight shone on his face enough for me to see reactions, as I said to him, "God loves you." He was on the verge of separation from his lovely and faithful wife. Infidelity had crept into his home, and he was the guilty party. The streetlight showed me a face that was almost contorted with inward pain, and he said, "Yes, I believe God loves me, but I am not so sure about the people of the church. They would never accept me." You see how empty the gospel sounds unless it is expressed in human beings.

Where is this face expressing God's love in the warp and woof of everyday things, where people live in the busyness of their lives? It has to be the face of a layman who bears his witness in the midst of life, whose soul has been sensitized by the Holy Spirit, who has become the channel of love, who with a dedicated imagination looks for the real needs of the person. If one is ever to do this it can be only as he yields himself, becoming the channel for downpouring, outpouring love.

## THE PARABLE

"The river will flow through a straw if the straw is in line with the river." I don't know who first said that, but it is one of life's most important truths. The human personality can become like a straw in the river, for the secret is not in the strength of the straw but in its alignment. The love of God will flow through a human personality if that personality is in line with the love of God—and the secret is not in strength, but in alignment.

Jesus spoke, as recorded in John 15, of branches in the vine, saying, "For just as the branch cannot bear any fruit unless it shares the life of the vine, so you can produce nothing unless you go on growing in me. I am the vine itself; you are the branches. It is the man who shares my life and whose life I share who proves fruitful" (John 15:4-5, Phillips). Love is a fruit of the Spirit, not one's personal fruit. He cannot generate love. It is a divine quality, to which he must yield and for which he must be a channel.

## FOR DISCUSSION

1. In what ways do you feel wrongly judged or in what ways do you think people may get the wrong impressions of you? Why is this?

2. Do you feel that you have the capacity to understand people very well? How do you evaluate yourself in this respect?

3. What are the qualities or abilities one must have to be such an understanding person?

4. Do you think there are many people who want to be offensive? If not, why are people sometimes so?

*Find people where they are,
listen to them, and find
areas of identification.*

# CHAPTER V

# Your Ministry

Your ministry is really Christ's own ministry through you. One has no power or right, as a human being, to offer from his own resources anything of redemption to his fellowman. The only redemptive ministry is the ministry of Christ himself. Our witness and service must be really the service of him who became our servant in order that we might become his servants.

"Let this mind be in you which was also in Christ Jesus" (Phil. 2:5). Phillips translates that passage: "Let Christ himself be your example as to what your attitude should be. For he, who had always been God by nature, did not cling to his prerogatives as God's equal, but stripped himself of all privilege by consenting to be a slave by nature and being born a mortal man" (vss. 5-7).

This is to say that our ministry must be in the same spirit and purpose and of the same *nature* as his ministry. His ministry was one of sacrificial love. "He gave himself." This was not a professional type of ministry, but a loving redemption. We discussed the nature of his love in Chapter II. Now we are saying that each person's ministry is to become the channel of that redemptive love. What, then, is your ministry?

### THE MINISTRY OF LISTENING

It is interesting to notice, according to Luke's account, that when Jesus as a lad of twelve years, remaining in Jerusalem when his parents were departing for Nazareth, went to the temple. Three days later they found him in the temple, "sitting among the teachers, listening to them and asking them questions; . . ." (Luke 2:46, RSV). Notice the order—he was listen-

51

ing before he asked questions. Was this a part of his preparation in depth? He listened! He heard what people had to say.
He heard what nature had to say. He opened his ears and his
mind to the values that were all around him. He spoke from the
depth because he *listened* in depth.

People of our time, in their busy, frantic, hectic lives, hardly
know how to listen, and they have little confidence that
anyone else really listens to them. We are very poor at communication in depth. There is, therefore, little real understanding. This is a part of the loneliness of our time. We know
little of how to listen and we have little experience in actually
being heard. A great feeling of loneliness overwhelms us.

This feeling of aloneness has deep psychological implications.
Dr. Camille Anderson was especially concerned about the psychology of children when she said, "The infant experiences a
basic depreciation in self-esteem if 'the one who knows best'
takes it for granted he doesn't know what he is talking about
or is not worth listening to. This might even account for the
failure of many adults to 'listen' to their bodies or to their
other feelings. Fatigue is brushed aside if the external authority
or the internalized censor demands more effort or better per-
formance. . . . It is deplorable to discover how many people
have never, during an entire lifetime, felt that they communi-
cated with any hope of being understood."[1] This is the deep
loneliness of our time, the feeling that no one really hears or
cares or understands or loves.

It is so easy—too easy—to say, "You can tell Jesus," but many
people do not know how to pray. They have no faith, no Lord
who is real to them. Religion is pretty fuzzy to most people.
They need a human being, a human hand, somebody good
enough, loving enough to keep a confidence, to witness their
self-exposure and never betray or condemn.

That man behind the face—he needs someone who will hear
him all the way through without his having to compete for

---

[1]*Beyond Freud.*

the floor or race for time. He needs someone who has the spirit of Jesus, who will understand.

Who will do this? The pastor? The psychologist? The doctor? Professional men do a great deal of listening, but time pressures are heavy and most people do not feel free to take so much time and open their hearts. What they need more than professional help is a friend who will listen.

The important thing in this kind of ministry to a person is not to say what you think but to hear what he thinks, for what he thinks is important. Not that it will convince you, but just because it is what *he* thinks. How he feels is important *just because he feels that way,* and because his own life is affected. Often people are helped tremendously just by someone listening—perhaps saying little or nothing, just listening.

### THE MINISTRY OF INTERCESSION

Intercession goes beyond listening, to involvement and care. To be an intercessor is to stand between, to plead for another. Have you any idea what it would mean for a distraught, burdened guilty person to hear a trusted Christian say, "I will pray for you."

Intercession follows in the principle of the vicarious. That is to say, it is taking the place of another person. It is to follow Christ in his care. It is to take upon yourself needs and burdens not your own.

The intercessor stands between. He is the connecting point between the need and the supply, the emptiness and the fullness. It is to be "plugged in," so to speak, to the life of Christ, and to be the transmitter of his love and power. Christians are literally the means through which Christ reaches people.

Ezekiel lived in a time when the people were apostate and unaware, and in a time of crisis he "wondered that there was no intercessor" (Isa. 59:16).

The Apostle Paul spoke in this vein when in 2 Corinthians 5:20 he said, "We are ambassadors for Christ, God making his appeal through us. We beseech you on behalf of Christ, be reconciled to God" (RSV). Such intercession follows Christ in identification with human need. It lifts a brother to him that his perfect work may be done.

When you enter into the needs of another with genuine care, you enter into Christ's own suffering and purpose. You enter into his vicarious work. You share in the "fellowship of his suffering," and this is your cross.

A dear friend of mine, and a great man of prayer, used to say, "When someone asks me to pray for him, the first thing I do is go alone and by a dedicated imagination I identify myself with his needs until I hurt in his hurt. Then I lift my friend and myself to God in simple faith. When peace comes to my own heart, I know my prayer is answered." That is intercession. It is more than casually mentioning a name in passing. It partakes of the nature of Christ's own ministry.

### THE MINISTRY OF WITNESSING

No attorney would tolerate for long a person in the witness chair who had only theories about what happened, or who was trying to relay the experience of somebody else. The important thing about a witness is that he speaks out of personal experience and actual firsthand knowledge. However limited a person's knowledge or understanding may be, he is valuable as a witness when he can say, "This I saw and heard."

The most powerful witness the Apostle John ever gave, perhaps, is recorded in his first epistle, "That which was from the beginning, which we have heard, which we have seen with our eyes, which we have looked upon and touched with our hands, concerning the word of life—the life was made manifest, and we saw it, and testify to it, and proclaim to you the eternal life which was with the Father and was made manifest to us—that which we have seen and heard we proclaim also to you, so that you may have fellowship with us; and our fellowship is with the Father and with his Son Jesus

Christ. And we are writing this that our joy may be complete"
(1 John 1:1-4, RSV).

Now there is a meaningful witness! "We have heard, . . . we
have seen, . . . we have looked upon . . . touched with our
hands. . . ." That is not a repeated rumor or secondhand story.
It is experience. Genuine witness comes from experience.

The most authoritative figures in the early church were the
apostles themselves. They were peculiarly qualified by the fact
that they had been with Jesus, that is, they spoke from firsthand knowledge. On one occasion people noted the difference
in them because "they had been with Jesus."

Witnessing is the confession of Christ. It is not taking a pose
as though one were superior. It is not so much to say, "I am
a Christian," as it is to say, "Christ is Lord." When Paul and
Barnabas in Iconium were lauded and praised unduly by the
people, their answer was a witness, "We also are men of
like passions with you, and preach unto you that you should
turn from these vanities unto the living God, which made
heaven, and earth, and the sea, and all things that are therein"
(Acts 14:15).

Witnessing is a man walking with his fellowman and with
God. It is to say, "I, too, am a man, but I have been with
God, and I have a message for you." A witness must lay hold
of *life* as well as of God. He is a bridge. And the witness
lays hold of life—especially if his witness goes along with a
ministry of listening and of intercession.

An elderly and saintly woman called on her pastor for prayer
when she was seriously sick. Faintly, she whispered, "I can't
have faith. I am too sick and too weak." The pastor asked,
"Can you believe in my prayers," and with emotion in her
voice she said, "Oh, yes, you know I can." In those two people,
experience came together, in the witness of one soul to another.
Faith strengthened faith. Fellowship in a person represented
the presence of Christ in healing power.

Witness is the exposure of your *own* needs and dependence
upon God. If you have had the experience, then through that

experience you will be able to speak to others. The sharing of experience may well be your ministry at the point where it most deeply touches the need of another person.

Witnessing is something far more than the reciting of a speech, like a magazine salesman working his way through college who dares not be interrupted for fear of losing his speech. It is more than pat answers or superficial conclusions. Real witness arises out of experience. This is why each of us has a priestly function in relation to other people. We stand between. We minister and serve through witness.

It is a tragedy when a person is not prepared for that witness. H. H. Hill told a story about an airman, badly smashed up, who was brought back from "somewhere in France" to a hospital in the north of England. After the doctor had patched him up as best he could, he turned to the airman in the next bed, "Say, mate, could you help a fellow with a bit of religion?" he asked. "Sorry, chum," the man replied, "but I am afraid I can't. But you will be all right. A lady visits here on Thursdays. She'll put you right." The young man answered, "Well, I may not be here on Thursday." After a while he turned to the fellow in the next bed, "I've been thinking," he said, "I don't know whether it is a bit out of the Bible or a part of a hymn, but some words kept running through my mind. Jesus said, 'Suffer little children to come to me.'" The fellow in the next bed answered, "Yeah, I think it is in the Bible all right, mate." There was another silence and then he said, "Well, if Jesus Christ wanted the children to come to him, do you think he would have me? I know jolly well I need Him. Anyway, I am going to ask Him." He pulled the sheet up over his head. That sheet never came down.[2]

## THE MINISTRY OF SIMPLE LOVE

An American novelist once told the story of a lovely lady who was married to a weak-willed man. After many years of

[2]*Prairie Pastor.*

life together, he revealed to her that he had been a thief
and was about to be exposed. It meant prison. He begged her
to leave him and get away from it all before she, too, became
involved. She looked at the pitiful face of this man
facing a prison sentence and asked, "Is it possible that we
have lived together so long and you have never learned that
my love for you is so great that what you have done is
my deed, too?" The loving loyalty of that wife was electric. A
broken-down man stooped to build his life with worn-out tools
because he had discovered the compelling power of a suffering love.[3]

Real love recognizes a certain identification with the person
who has lost his way. You look upon a man with criticism and
say, "How coarse he is." Look at him with scorn and say, "How
small he is." But look through the mirror of truth and love and
say, "How like me my brother is."

The first and most indispensable rule that we must never
break is, "Judge not." When you hold a condemning opinion of
someone, it not only holds that one in bondage, but it holds
you in bondage, as well. No man can judge another without
judging himself. If a man were perfectly free from sin, he
would be too pure to see sin in anyone else. When one sees
the evil in another, it brings out that evil. If he sees
the best in others, they will become better persons in his presence.

It is said that Balzac's profound knowledge of human nature
caused the great novelist to fancy himself as an expert at
reading character in handwriting. One day an old woman
brought him a little boy's copybook and said, "Master, what do
you think of this child's possibilities?" Balzac studied the
scrawly, untidy handwriting. "Well," said Balzac, "this child is
slovenly and profoundly stupid. I fear he will never amount
to anything." And then the woman cried, "But Master, that
copybook was your very own when you were a little boy in

---

[3]Told by K. Morgan Edwards.

school." Is there not profound wisdom in Jesus' words, "Judge not that you be not judged"?

Love is to see through the exterior like a doctor sees beyond the symptoms to the nature of the disease. It is to try to understand a person, to respect his inner uniqueness. It is not a kind of possessiveness which would make someone else over into the pattern we desire, but, rather, with creative faith help him to discover himself and his own true stride.

One thing Jesus taught us was that every person we meet is a human soul with dignity, and that we are guilty of gross inhumanity when we snub or abuse him. The primary joy of life is acceptance, approval, the sense of appreciation and companionship with our human comrades. Someone has said, "Love is dependent on an inner beauty of the mind and soul. Its depths have never been plumbed; its limit has never been reached."

The words of Francis of Assisi are immortal. They represent the heart cry of every truly Christian person motivated by love:

> Lord, make me an instrument of Thy peace.
>   Where there is hatred, let me sow love;
>   Where there is injury, pardon;
>   Where there is doubt, faith;
>   Where there is despair, hope;
>   Where there is darkness, light;
>   And where there is sadness, joy.
> O Divine Master, grant that I may not so much seek
>   To be consoled as to console;
>   To be understood as to understand;
>   To be loved as to love;
>   For it is in giving that we receive;
>   It is in pardoning that we are pardoned,
>   And it is in dying that we are born to eternal life.

### The Support of Fellowship

Fortunately, you need not go it alone. Your ministry does not stand alone. It is united with that of many other Christian laymen. It is strengthened by their example and by their fellowship.

God has chosen to work through fellowship. The baptism of the Holy Spirit on Pentecost came when they were united "all together in one place." The greatest power of the church has been manifest when there was deep unity and fellowship.

We are touching here something that is as old as Christianity itself. Jesus gathered a small group of disciples about him for intensive quest. This is perhaps the most significant thing he did, outside the atoning work itself.

A week of experience with Christian young people in Egypt convinced me that these young people, living in a culture far from congenial to their Christian convictions, found much greater strength and help in their fellowship together than is customarily felt in nominal Christian America. They needed one another. They found help and strength together. Fellowship had great meaning.

But to every person, Christian fellowship, with the power of Christian example and mutual inspiration, is a corrective of extreme importance. It helps set our values straight; improper conduct is confronted by example, and the sense of aloneness is confronted by meaningful relatedness with other people.

The church must be an open fellowship, not closed. Some churches are like a tight little circle of people standing together, facing inward—exclusive and snobbish, with no real redemptive purpose at all. Some are super-righteous, with a word of condemnation for anyone who differs, relentless and unforgiving in their attitude. It is said that John Oglethorpe said to John Wesley once, "I never forgive." Wesley's reply was prompt and devastating, "Then I hope, sir, you never sin."

When will we learn that the church of Christ is intended to be a loving and redemptive fellowship? The ministry of each person depends upon this truth. For you cannot stand alone or bear your witness alone. Your own ministry is powerfully strengthened or virtually canceled out by the kind of spirit in the local congregation.

FOR DISCUSSION

1. Have you ever had a friend to whom you felt you could reveal your whole self without fear of being rejected, condemned, or your confidence betrayed, and in whose presence you were utterly at ease?

2. Have you ever been that kind of person? Would a troubled person feel free to come to you? Can you listen?

3. Have you ever really prayed the intercessory prayer or been an intercessory person? Do you want to be?

4. What are some of the areas in which a real and effective witness can take place?

5. What do we mean by "Identification" with another person?

*To introduce a friend to*
*Christ is the highest*
*privilege of man.*

# CHAPTER VI

# *Friend to Friend*

The highest privilege a person can know is to lead a friend to his Eternal Friend. At this point one should stop and remove his shoes, for he is standing on holy ground. We have been considering the priesthood of all believers, the fact that each Christian is a minister and a priest in the sense that he stands, so to speak, between another person and God. This is the highest expression of the priesthood of all believers—leading another person to a knowledge of Jesus Christ as Savior and Lord.

The story of the gospel is that of how God the Eternal Person sought persons through the person of Jesus Christ. The work of the church might be described as God the Eternal Person seeking persons through persons. There is the collective ministry of the church as a whole, but there must always be this individual application—a person-to-person ministry.

Evangelism must move from the periphery of the church to its center. This is the church's main track. This is the central purpose. If we cannot lead people to genuine conversion, we have lost the right to be called Christian. If we are not evangelistic in this true and deep sense, we have no right to be called evangelical. One's experience with Jesus Christ must be capable of contagion and duplication. It is not merely Christendom but Christ, not churchification but salvation. This zeroes right in on the individual and the vitality of his Christian life, not only the ordained minister but the layman as well.

## The Meaning of Priesthood

Jesus Christ is our High Priest. He stands between each of us and eternal salvation, the Mediator between God and man. He is also the sacrifice, the Lamb slain from the foundation of

the world. He made God available to man. He leads man to
God. He is the Son of God and the Son of man. As the
epitome of divine love, he effected the Atonement, bringing
God and man together in himself.

But not many people realize that Jesus, who was called of
God as High Priest, was not descended from the priestly tribe
of Aaron. He was not of the Aaronic priesthood, which was the
only Jewish priesthood of that day. The writer of Hebrews
speaks of him as "the apostle and high priest of our confession" (Heb. 3:1, RSV). Later he said, "For we have not a
high priest who is unable to sympathize with our weaknesses,
but one who in every respect has been tempted as we are, yet
without sinning. Let us then with confidence draw near to the
throne of grace, that we may receive mercy and find grace to
help in time of need" (4:15-16, RSV). But the writer spoke
of him as a high priest in an unusual sense: "So also Christ did
not exalt himself to be made a high priest, but was appointed
by him who said to him, 'Thou art my Son, today I have
begotten thee'; as he says also in another place, 'Thou art a
priest forever, after the order of Melchizedek'" (5:5-6, RSV).

In a very real sense Jesus was essentially and eternally
"priest"—the priest from whom all our priesthood derives. He
had to exercise his priestly ministry, however, outside the established priestly order. To laymen what limitless opportunities
this opens up—and what tremendous demands!

The Apostle Paul urges us to present our bodies a "living
sacrifice" in order that we may "prove" the will of God. Can
your mind take this in? Each Christian is, in a sense, a priest,
and in a sense a sacrifice. Through him the ministry of Christ
is continued. Whatever the circumstances or conditions of our
lives, we must exercise this priesthood while united with him
and in him in a spiritually organic relationship as the branch
is in the vine. (See John 15.)

There is a common sacrificial pattern, therefore, which
emerges for all of us. The details must be filled in in terms of
the uniqueness in each one's personality, abilities, and frame

of living. In all circumstances one is to be offered where he is, in his "world," and by his own choosing and free will, whatever his work or profession, whatever his family situation, and whatever his limitations. He has what someone has called the "interior priesthood" of concern for other persons, and this is indeed an eloquent and potent force.

## THE LAYMAN AS A PRIEST

Let us, in one paragraph, gather up several things we have been saying. In the framework of one's vocation and daily living, by the exercise of personal friendship, through mutual interests, skills, and concerns, each of us is to follow after the ministry of Jesus Christ. By looking upon each person in depth and with an understanding love, you begin with that which is essential and basic in man, rather than, in the name of religion, judging because of appearances. It is to place your mind and body, your knowledge and skills, your interests and experiences upon the altar of willing sacrifice, and by a dedicated imagination find ways to minister to your fellowman. This is the most valid ministry you can have. Of course, the ordained minister does this in preaching. There it must necessarily be more generally applied and in more generalized terms. But in a very real sense a message from God comes through the heart and experience of a person. And the greatest sermon a man ever preached is the sermon of his own life and spirit.

To illustrate the validity and centrality of this personal ministry, a beautiful story was told of Dr. John A. Broadus, the scholar and homiletics professor:

In his younger days he was converted to Christ in the town in which he lived. Next day he went to one of his schoolmates, Sandy Jones, a red-haired chap, and said to him, "I wish you would be a Christian; won't you?" And Sandy said: "Well, I don't know. Perhaps I will." And sure enough, one night in the little church, Sandy Jones accepted Christ. Straightway he stalked across that little meetinghouse, held out his hand, and said, "I thank you, John; I thank you, John."

Dr. Broadus went forth from that little town and became a great scholar, a great exegete and theological president. Every summer when he went home this red-haired old farmer, in his plain clothes, would come up, stick out his great, bony hand, and say, "Howdy, John. Thank you, John. . . ."

And they say that when Dr. Broadus lay dying, his family about him, he said; "I rather think the sound sweetest to my ears in Heaven, next to the welcome of Him whom not having seen, I have tried to love and serve, will be the welcome of Sandy Jones, as he will thrust out his great hand and say, "Howdy, John! Thank you, John. . . ."[1]

It might be properly said that when a man allows this personal ministry to die and be forgotten in his own life, any other ministry, professional or otherwise, is something less than valid.

## THE IMPORTANCE OF AWARENESS

No one very wise will seriously suggest that you make a bold and frontal approach to every person you meet, to "witness for Christ." Observation teaches us that such an approach would type a person as superficial, as well as doctrinaire and dogmatic. If you are to win another person, you must be concerned with the impression you make, and, in a sense, put your best foot forward. If you are concerned with the other person, you must be concerned about what he thinks and how he feels, not for your own sake but for his. In the world of business and marketplace, we know this quite well. But for some strange reason, "witnessing for Christ" has been associated with the strictly overt approach—obvious and sometimes downright offensive.

The Christian needs to pray for sensitivity and awareness, alertness to human needs and opportunity, adroitness in influencing a conversation in the direction where a witness can be given for Christ in a quiet way, without ostentation or embarrassment. Humility here is golden.

The essence of good teaching or getting an idea across to someone else is to begin by seeing through his eyes, sensing

---

[1]From the *Watchman Examiner*.

his thought and feeling. It is, so to speak, going to his "world."

Jesus taught us this, starting as he did with circumstances and experiences that people well knew. Beginning with their world of experience and thought he gave them spiritual lessons. He deeply loved people. Therefore, he was aware of their thinking and their needs.

Most of us are unaware. We are preoccupied with our own "world" of concerns, ambitions, and fears. And because of our preoccupation we are impervious and, for all practical purposes, anonymous and neutral, so far as affecting any other life is concerned.

Traveling back and forth across the country, I have had experiences both ways. On a train or plane I have been tempted to settle down with a book or with my own thoughts, paying little or no attention to anyone around me. At other times I have deliberately prayed for sensitivity and awareness to the needs of people about me, and always opportunities come. No one can describe a set line of approach to reach another person. In every case it is different. There is no substitute for awareness. It was said of Ernie Pyle that he was like a microphone among the military personnel of World War II, highly sensitive to their thinking, their feeling, their morale, and their needs. Christians ought to be like that!

### PLANTING THE SEED

There is no seed so powerful as a quiet, humble example in Christian living. What a man *is* speaks louder than any words he can say, and his words will be empty if they are not backed up by the right kind of example. His witness will be powerfully augmented or mercilessly negated by what he is, how he lives, how he reacts under pressure, his standard of ethics, his trustworthiness, the very spirit of his life.

Next in importance, perhaps, is friendliness and outgoingness. There are many good people who live in a shell. Their "world" is closed in. They are not communicative. While the power of a Christian example is not necessarily diminished because of silence, it is too often accompanied by an ingrownness and a kind of removal from other people. The Christian example needs to reach out, to actually touch someone else. A great many people are willing to confine their Christian witness to a proper example, but we cannot be satisfied with neutrality and passivity. Anonymous Christians don't change the course of events. You must plant the seed in word and in the outreach of friendship, as well as by your deeds.

A sublime story was related to me by a personal friend. He was traveling by plane across the southern states when a young steward noticed on his ticket that he was a clergyman, and told him this story. On a previous flight, some weeks before, he was coming through the aisle when a hand reached out and touched his arm. It turned out to be a layman who was, nonetheless, an administrative officer for his church. He told him in just a few moments, frankly and candidly, of God's love for him. He was so moved by this Christian witness that while in flight he gave his heart to God. He and his fiancee determined, as a result, that their home would be a Christian one. People who know that man have said that he bears this kind of witness across the length and breadth of the country. Talk about approach—that is blunt, but kind and genuine, because it came from a heart conditioned by love for people and a life transparently dedicated and Christian.

There was a housewife who felt there was nothing, really, that she could do as a worthwhile expression of her Christian commitment. One morning in prayer she asked God to show her what she could do. When later she was washing dishes at the sink she looked out the window and saw a moving van stop at a house across the street. Then, almost like a revelation, she saw her opportunity to do a kindness and to welcome the new people as neighbors. About noon, when their kitchen appliances were not yet connected and they would not be able to prepare a noon meal, she took hot pie and hot coffee and welcomed them to the neighborhood. Needless to say, she made new friends and found opportunity eventually to witness. This became a pattern of her life. Who can estimate the power of such a witness? She began with a hot pie and ended by warming hearts!

Seedtime may begin in an act of kindness, the right word of greeting, or even by simply meeting another person's eyes squarely.

## CULTIVATION IS VITAL

The most important cultivating we ever do is by prayer. One's own life is transformed when he begins to pray earnestly and seriously for another person, when his prayer takes on an intercessory quality, when he puts himself in another person's place, tries to see through his eyes, and feel something of the need of his life.

For one thing, this is the most valuable spiritual exercise for his own life. He begins to see himself as a channel and an instrument of God. The flaws show up and he sees more than ever the importance of a transparently Christian life. As he prays his own attitudes will change to deep empathy with the person that he is trying to reach. He will be less condescending and more loving, less cocksure and more humble.

It is interesting to observe how Jesus proceeded in speaking to the woman of Samaria. First, he found her dominant interest —water. Second, he raised that to a higher issue—living water. Third, he came to grips with the moral problem which was troubling her life. Fourth, when she raised the smokescreen of whether to worship there in the mountain or in Jerusalem, he focused attention on the higher personal issue of worshiping God in spirit and truth. Fifth, she was so impressed as to recognize him, the Christ. And, finally, she herself became an evangelist. There is an example for you—and a pattern.

Cultivation takes place through continued friendship, and also through fellowship, as you bring the resources of Christian fellowship to bear by inviting a friend into the circle of Christian friends. There are hundreds of opportunities for this. But the tendency is to confine friendships to other Christian people with whom you are in agreement—a nice compact little circle!

Someone has spoken of "coffee cup evangelism." Others speak of "friendship evangelism" or "fellowship evangelism." They are all talking about cultivation as the opportunity permits and as circumstances would seem to indicate. One of the best places for cultivation is in your own home, when you invite people as guests. There you can set the atmosphere and somewhat control the conditions. You can generally make the situation conducive to witnessing in depth. But your imagination has to get on the altar. If you were courting a girl or cultivating a business prospect, you would have ideas on what to do. Why not for an effective Christian witness?

### FAMILY TO FAMILY

Happy indeed is that family that assumes such responsibility together in the winning of neighbors and friends. Family worship takes on a very different and great meaning when you begin to pray for somebody else. Fun and fellowship can have a depth of purpose when this is your goal.

In some ways you might say that it is easier to win a family, as a family, than to win an individual as an individual. The feelings of love and solidarity in the family circle seem to invite the presence of Christ. The parents' sense of responsibility leads them, often, to an awareness of their need of Christ. The open, eager attitude of children and their interest in many activities in the church school will work in your favor. Friendships which develop between different members of two families tend to corroborate and strengthen the Christian witness.

As your family reaches out to neighbors or friends, even your children will sense the thrill of spiritual adventure. Family worship will have vastly more meaning as you pray for them. The power of your love is felt through a thousand little things and incidents. This is a real adventure in family living.

On one occasion, after such concern for a neighbor, my little daughter ran up behind me one evening when I was raking the lawn. She urged me to come down the street a few doors where a new family had just moved in. I went along (keeping the lawn broom in my hand so they would know I didn't always dress that way) and she marched right up on the porch, knocked at the door, and introduced me like a little veteran. Later she said, "I *knew* you'd want to meet them, Daddy." She was eight years old.

There are so many natural, normal, socially acceptable ways to win people for Christ, not only in the framework of vocation but of family life and neighborhood relationships. In countless ways that only your own imagination will uncover, you can be the instrument of outgoing love.

### THE VESTIBULE OF THE CHURCH

The age group or class fellowship bringing together as it does people of mutual interests, of similar age and experience, and constituting as it does a natural social unit, is about the finest medium through which you can introduce your friends to the total fellowship of the church and ultimately to Christ. It can be a kind of vestibule. Often this begins in a social occasion or class meeting where you have a natural opportunity to invite your friends. It is an ideal occasion to make them acquainted with other members of the group. It affords you the opportunity to enlist the help and the Christian example of others, throwing around your friend a wall of Christian fellowship and concern. Often the mere lack of acquaintance or the feeling of being ill-at-ease prevents a person from finding his way into the fellowship of Christian people. This gives you the opportunity to melt the barriers and help them feel at home.

Later, perhaps, it will come quite natural to invite your friends to the class sessions themselves. Here the group discussion, if properly conducted, raises questions related to life. It is, of course, very important for class discussions to be meaningful and vital, and to be conducted in a constructive manner and spirit. (Negative and critical discussions can ruin everything!) The larger the group involved, the more general must be the discussion or lecture. Smaller groups, therefore, are often more vital, for they get closer to the real issues in the lives of people present. If a class discussion presents the gospel of Christ positively and in relevant, current terms, it will have a great deal to do with winning your friends to Christ.

Then there is the power of group prayer. If the members of your class are praying people—and they should be—the effect of united group prayer is enormous. Thus the interest or age groups within the church can be powerful means of outreach. At the same time, the group becomes a corroborating and supportive power for the individual Christian layman as he bears his witness through friendship and natural affinities with other people.

Perhaps something should be said of the "quest" or interest group. This is generally a group of dedicated and disciplined people who think together and earnestly seek for greater knowledge, for greater spiritual maturity, and for greater power of witness. In the last few years there has been a groundswell of interest among laymen in this type of approach. What does it mean to be Christian in my business or profession? How can we bear effective Christian witness in the midst of business, political, and professional life? Any sincere Christian layman will be wise to become a part of such an intensive and questing fellowship.

Such intensive groups have powerful outreach, as well. More than one life has been transformed by being drawn into such a quest group. Many of them reach across church lines, are formed on a neighborhood basis, or out of acquaintance and friendship.

### MEET THE MASTER

When that time comes, as we pray it will, that you have the privilege of taking a person by the hand, so to speak, and saying, "Meet my Lord," you will have entered into the highest privilege known to a human being. Winning a person to Christ is not "making him over" according to your design, but rather leading him as he is to the Savior, in the light of whose presence his individuality will bloom as at the same time his guilt and fear are removed, and as he comes to accept fully the great love of God through Christ.

This is the point at which you lead your friend to the adequate High Priest, the great Mediator, the Savior. In a sense you have had a ministry, but your highest ministry is in introducing a friend to him.

One humble, quiet, godly man was able to lead one young man after another to Christ. He was very hesitant of speech, and when asked what he said to these young men, he wept, saying, "I don't know what to say." When pressed for what he actually did say, this was his answer: "I just tell them, 'I'll go with you.'" Can you think of anything better to say? The witnessing had already been done.

You don't force a response. You don't coerce a person into being a Christian any more than a florist pries open the bud to make a flower bloom. Someplace I ran across this story:

She picked a flower from the window box that stood near the door and examined it. It was a petunia that earlier in the day had been a wide star of deep purple but now was folded in upon itself, its petals furled.

"If you wanted to make this flower open," she said, "there would be two ways. You could force its petals apart. But if you did that too hard you'd tear it. The other way would be like this." She held the flower in the doorway. "If it was in the sunlight long enough, it would open by itself."

"All right, so what?"

"It's like that with healing—don't you see? If you force your will upon it too hard, you tear it down. But if you provide the right kind of light and warmth and nourishment, you can bring about the healing of its own accord."

It isn't a case of ability, primarily. It is one of dedicated imagination and, above all, true Christian love.

### For Discussion

1. Have you ever led another person to Christ? How?
2. Who influenced you most in your acceptance of Christ as your Savior? How?
3. Are you interested—would you be willing—to become a deep and real winner of other people?
4. When do you plan to begin?

*"You must serve one
another, each with the
talent he has received,
as efficient stewards of
God's varied grace."—
1 Peter 4:10, Moffatt*

# CHAPTER VII

# For the Common Good

The church is a Christ-centered brotherhood. It is a mutually
supporting fellowship of people whose primary responsibility is
bearing witness in the world. It might be said that laymen
are the church's projection into the world.

In this chapter we shall be concerned about our ministry
to one another within the fellowship of the church, with the
full understanding that this is not our only responsibility, and
that it is not enough simply to do "church work." Nonetheless
the church as an institution and as a fellowship is a tremendously powerful witness in the world. Through it you have
the corroboration and underscoring of your own witness. To it
you back up for strength and instruction. You receive much from
the church. You owe much, also, to the church. "Each receives
his manifestation of the Spirit for the common good," wrote
Paul. ". . . the various members should have a common concern for one another" (1 Cor. 12:7, 25, Moffatt).

There needs to be an interpenetration between the church
and the world. The perspective, the training, the spiritual per-
ceptiveness, and awareness one receives in the fellowship of
Christians and under Christian teaching must be given expression in the "common ventures" of life. Conversely, the skills,
the know-how, the perspective and viewpoint from one's experience in the "common ventures" are needed in the church,
for it has business relationships, it is an educational institution,
and it has public relations concerns. The layman, therefore,

has much to give within the structure of the church for its guidance in the full-orbed ministry to people and its relationships in the community life.

Perhaps the church needs to be less "worldly minded" and more "world-minded." It needs to be aware of where people live and what they think. The layman can, therefore, bear a witness *from* the midst of life, as well as *in* the midst of life.

## The Ministry of Christ Continues

Please remember that Jesus Christ did not speak from a swivel chair, or necessarily from a platform. He did not merely live, to use Sam Walter Foss's well-known expression, "in a house by the side of the road." He lived *in* the road, with people. He was footsore and weary. He felt the heat of the day upon his head and the cold dew of the night upon his face. He met people where they were—suffering, bleeding, hateful, guilty, discouraged, and battered by life. He was, in the finest sense, a man of the *world*. He was acquainted with everyday things and common problems. He was world minded as well as spiritually minded.

The church is portrayed in the New Testament as the "body of Christ." The church is to the eternal spirit of Christ today what his physical body was to his spirit. It is his habitation, the channel through which he works and ministers in the world. The church is his continuing ministry.

We therefore conceive of the church in the functional terms of movement, life, ministry, and sharing. The institutional aspect is a means to the end. The real point of it all is ministering in the midst of mankind.

The church is the gathering and scattering of the people of God—gathering for worship, learning, and spiritual growth; scattering for witness and ministry, permeating society at every level, and, like the apostles of old, we ought to go "everywhere preaching the Word." The redeemed community is a redeeming community. Evangelism is built in!

The church of the first generation after Christ was based on an inspired membership, an inspired ministry, and inspired government. Above all, the church on earth and in heaven was no mere human society, but the living body of Christ, the purpose of which was to carry forward his ministry of love.

While each person has his own individual ministry, he is also united in ministry with others. He is, in a sense, alone, yet not alone. In a conversation with Alice Ehlers, a harpsichordist, Albert Schweitzer remarked: "Always listen to the inner voices of Bach's music. Each voice lives its own life, dependently and independently at the same time. If you will look at Bach's music that way, letting each voice sing out its own beauty, I am sure you cannot fail."[1] What a splendid description of what transpires in our mutual ministry. Here is a man, independent of Christ and the church from one point of view but hopelessly dependent from another. And here, even, is Christ, independent of man, dwelling not in temples made by human hands, and yet dependent upon man for the carrying out of his purposes. He is listening for your strain of melody. And you must listen to his. What music we can make when we submit to him, the Conductor, and yield our own instruments to his direction!

Thus the nature and mission of the church are inseparable. The evangelistic mission belongs to the nature of the church. To be a Christian is to be an evangelist and that is not optional. The church, its Lord, and its mission are all one. To be separated from one is to be separated from all. The church is God's continuing redemptive activity in the world.

## THE WORK OF THE HOLY SPIRIT

"What is the Holy Spirit?" a layman was asked. He answered, with disarming and disturbing candor, "Well, to me it is a kind of gray, fuzzy, oblong blur." If that kind of fuzziness of understanding can be construed as typical in any degree, then it is indeed no wonder that the church is without the power she

---

[1]Gifford Millard in *The Pulpit*, August, 1948.

needs in such a time as this, for the Holy Spirit is the life-giving power of the church, and the church is the community of the Holy Spirit. According to the Bible, the fruits of the Spirit—love, joy, peace, longsuffering, gentleness, goodness, faith, meekness, and temperance—are the very characteristics most needed in the church today. But how can we have the fruits of the Spirit without the Spirit? And how can we have the Holy Spirit without more clear teaching concerning him and his work? This is a truly great need in the church.

Jesus talked most about the Holy Spirit between the time when he instituted the Lord's Supper and knelt to wash the feet of his followers, and the time when he went to the cross. What Jesus said is recorded by the sensitive Apostle John, who apparently was more aware of the deeper aspects of Jesus' teaching than were most of the others. In his gospel, chapters 14, 15, and 16, John records Jesus as speaking frequently about the Holy Spirit. In chapter 17 he records the so-called high-priestly prayer, in which Christ prayed so earnestly for his followers. A careful study of these four chapters, along with references to him in the epistles, will reveal something of what the Holy Spirit does in the church.

He, the Spirit of Truth, is the great Teacher, to lead us into all truth. No place do you read that the Holy Spirit is to teach us automatically or give us knowledge without any discipline of our own. We must study and cooperate with him. But he is the great illuminator, making truth come alive, bringing it to remembrance, making it real and vital.

He is the great Cleanser. Along with his teaching and the understanding we receive, the conscience is quickened and one is made sensitive and aware. A great cleansing takes place when you receive him by faith, and this cleansing work goes on as you gain understanding and spiritual maturity.

He is the great Comforter, not in the sense of making you comfortable and at ease, but in the true sense of giving inner fortitude, for this means fortification from within. It means that He who is within you is greater than he that is in the world.

He is the great Giver of Power—power to live victoriously, power to win people for Christ, power of contagion, power that comes by sincere love and faith. The personality once canceled out by inner fear, guilt, conflict, and tension, can be increasingly set free by the power of the Holy Spirit and a life dedicated to his holy purpose.

The Holy Spirit *guides* one into paths of service, and this is really the crowning of his work, for the continuing redemptive purpose of Christ is carried out by him. According to Jesus, he penetrates and convicts, accompanying the teaching of the gospel, intimately associated in the proclamation of the Word. Jesus promised this in words to his disciples. "When he comes, he will convince the world of the meaning of sin, of true goodness and of judgment. He will expose their sin because they do not believe in me; he will reveal true goodness for I am going away to the Father and you will see me no longer; and he will show them the meaning of judgment, for the spirit which rules this world will have been judged" (John 16:8, 9, Phillips).

You have the assurance, then, that you are not alone. Christian witness is much more than pitting your own small voice against the din and noise of the world. Directed by the Spirit, your witness takes on another dimension. His truth and his spirit have a tremendous penetrating quality. The Holy Spirit alone, in the very nature of the case, produces the fruits of the Spirit. No one would deny the need for these fruits in his own life, and no one could question that these are the characteristics so needed if we are to perform a ministry of love.

## GIFTS OF THE SPIRIT

In Romans 12, 1 Corinthians 12, and Ephesians 4, you read about the church in a peculiar and wonderful sense, for it is pictured as being like the human body where the members of the body have vital functions as they do in the human body. They are interdependent. They contribute to one another and to the welfare of the body as a whole.

The special qualifications of members are spoken of as "gifts" of the spirit, and you get the distinct impression that the Holy Spirit is at work in the church as a corporate body and through its fellowship. No one has a "corner" on him. He is available to all. There is no service that one can render to God except as he serves his fellowman, for all these gifts are *serving* gifts. They are not for demonstration purposes. They are not to prove how spiritual one is, but to carry out his mission in the world.

The word is "charisma," which means "gift." Sometimes theologians speak of the charismatic nature of the church. This charismatic is not a passing phase, but a permanent characteristic of the church at its best.

One man dared to say in a group meeting, "There is something about Christ that is incomplete until we are in him. He fills us so that we may fulfill him. Redeemed humanity becomes incarnate divinity. A person cannot find himself as a Christian except he finds himself in the body, and Christ cannot express himself in the world except through his body, the church." This is saying, in a very deep and almost frightening sense, that the whole church is the continuing ministry of Christ. It is his spirit and purpose, his redeeming power, present in the world, and the church has meaning and character precisely and only because the living presence of the Holy Spirit gives it character and meaning. Without this living presence, a mere group of people does not constitute the church. The genius of the church lies in *relationship.* Jesus said, "Where two or three are gathered together in my name, there am I in the midst of them" (Matt. 18:20).

Each person, therefore, is to find his place of service under the guidance of the Holy Spirit, and through the exercising of his "gift" contribute to the life and strength of the entire body.

## Unity Is Sacred

To many people Christian unity seems an optional matter and not a very serious option, at that. But look at the Bible.

Christ promised unity (John 10:16). He prayed for it (John 17:11-23). He died for it (John 11:50; Eph. 2:13-16). It was experienced in the early church (Acts 4:32). They had fellowship together (Acts 2:42). They accepted the same basic truths and unity mounted above the divisions then rampant (Gal. 3:28; Col. 3:11; Eph. 4). That unity resulted in great power (Acts 4:32-33).

Such unity is of the heart and rooted in personal experience (Jude 3). It depends upon having the same spirit (1 Cor. 12:13). It is being of one mind and one spirit (1 Cor. 1:10; Phil. 2:2; Rom. 15:6).

A careful study of the foregoing passages from the Holy Scriptures will establish clearly that the lowering of barriers between man and fellowman is coincident with, and a part of, the acceptance of Christ and the change of heart which results.

Chester Warren Quimby explores of the writings of Paul the Apostle in relation to practical unity, saying:

> This is the wonder of Paul. . . . in Romans he has set down principles which, if heeded, would have forestalled this whole sinful business (of division). Look at these principles again! Really see them, for they are for the salvation of the church.
> Let there be no arrogance one over another in matters of conscientious dispute.
> Never pass censorious judgment upon another's scruples.
> Put no pressure on one whereby he denies his conscience.
> Let each man do as before God seems to him right.
> Remember, the essentials are right relations, peace and joy.
> In all disputes seek not self-justification, but unity.
> Look upon all men with whom you differ as brothers for whom Christ died.
> Remember, Christ pleased not himself.
> Let everything be done in love.[2]

Commenting further on the writings of the Apostle, he said:

> Paul was pleading for unity, harmony and fellowship. He was not pleading for uniformity. Never does he say, "Come to an agreement." He was against scorning the vegetable eater for not tasting meat. He did not require the liberal Sabbath observer to change his no-

---

[2]*The Great Redemption* (New York: The Macmillan Company, 1950), p. 193.

tions. He asked only that those in disagreement live together in harmony and mutual helpfulness. . . . Paul believed in diversity, but never in disunity.[3]

Harmony is not all one color, but different colors, which complement and accentuate one another, bringing out the more subtle shades. Harmony is not one sound or tone, but different tones, which enhance one another, bringing depth, color, and beauty. Unity is not all one ability, viewpoint, or experience, but many, blended into varied and limitless harmony. Each gift, temperament, or viewpoint is tempered, modified, lifted up, and used as a part of God's design. Unity is not everyone thinking alike. (Where everyone thinks alike, perhaps no one is thinking very much.) Unity is not the absence of differences, but the spirit of love in which our differences become contributions, rather than points of conflict. We are enriched and taught by one another.

It ought to be understood that this unity is not simply that we liked one another's looks and decided to get together. It is rooted solidly in the redemption of Christ. Unity is possible only "in" him.

Finally, the unity of Christ's people is a testimony to the world. Hear Jesus praying, "But it is not for these alone that I pray, but for those also who through their words put their faith in me; may they all be one: as thou, Father, art in me, and I in thee, so also may they be in us, that the world may believe that thou didst send me" (John 17:20-21, NEB). Division among Christians cancels out much of their influence in the world and nullifies their witness.

## SENT INTO THE WORLD

In the same prayer, at the same time, that Jesus prayed for the unity of his followers he prayed also as follows: "I pray thee, not to take them out of the world, but to keep them from the evil one. They are strangers in the world, as I am.

---

[3]*Ibid.*, p. 192.

Consecrate them by the truth; thy word is truth. As thou hast sent me into the world, I have sent them into the world, and for their sake I now consecrate myself, that they too may be consecrated by the truth" (vss. 15-19, NEB).

Such penetration into the world is the real ministry. The church must direct people to a communion of the spirit with the people of God, but also it must realize community amid the affairs of men. The church is somewhat like a fishing fleet, where from the mother ship the individual boats are daily launched to carry each fisherman to his task. To the mother ship each boat returns regularly, bringing its prizes, and the fisherman replenishes his supplies and renews his strength. You must find the balance of giving and receiving, of worship and witness. You receive that you may also share.

So you have a ministry within the church as well as in the marketplace. The gifts of the Spirit are "for the common good." Thus the church as a body edifies itself and builds itself up in love, and we receive from one another strength and inspiration so that we may effectively bear our witness again in the world of affairs. This saves the church from being unreal and helps b r i d g e the great gap between what Dr. Samuel Shoemaker called the "self-conscious churchman and the lost-worldlings." Perhaps the main reason why many thoughtful people manifest an aversion to the church is not to be found in a particular dislike for her worship or a rejection of her teaching. It is more often found in the sense of *unreality* and irrelevancy in the church's life.

The church is intended to be a spiritual minority in the midst of majority, a dynamic nucleus, an object lesson in human brotherhood. And in the very nature of the case, this speaks to the deepest ills and needs of men. Our greatest problem is not cancer, but rancor. Ignorance, prejudice, hostility, and superstition still abound. Injustice is deep-rooted in much of our economic and social systems. We advance technologically but we break down at the point of human relations. We can travel over the earth and sea, and we can burrow beneath the earth for its minerals. We can fly above the earth and even probe space beyond the earth, but we don't know very well how to live in harmony *on* the earth. As L. K. Bishop once said, "The most difficult field to which man can set his mind in our generation is this field of human engineering. It is far easier to labor with test tubes, minerals, or medicine. Just as we attack the problem of cancer, so we must enter the field of bigotry, hate, and prejudice. We must determine to find the source of human strife, discord and hostility even as we are determined to find the source of polio infection."

In the church we must overcome the scantiness of our knowledge of the world of today, and what really goes on under the surface. We must reform our own spirits and attitudes and, if necessary, our inherited structure, to make room for new vitality, so that the church will be less a sacramentalized form and more a *sanctified force.*

## You Need the Church

The man who doesn't have time to go to church is like an automobile that doesn't have time to stop for gasoline. It is said that a certain pastor was grieved over a backslider who had once been a faithful Christian and a regular attendant at the house of worship. He went to the man's home and found him sitting before an open fire. Without saying a word the minister took up the tongs, lifted a glowing coal from the fire, and laid it aside on the hearthstone. In silence they watched it die out. Said the backslider, "You needn't say a word, Pastor. I get the message."

You often see on a ticket or coupon these words, "Void if detached." Those words should be stamped on the foreheads of all Christians. Whenever an individual loses touch with the work, worship, and fellowship of the church, he is in grave danger of falling into doubts, neutrality, and even moral decay.

John F. Locke told the story of a friend of college days who had studied medicine at the University of Paris and then had gone into French Equatorial Africa for fourteen years as a missionary. He had stopped to visit with him and said, "As we talked of the church he said the best definition he had ever found of the church was in Matthew 18:20, 'Where two or three are gathered together in my name, there I am in the midst of them.' He pointed out that such a group meets *together* for a *Christian purpose*, and that *He* is there *in the midst*. He said that often on preaching tours in remote areas there would be much interest but a year later, unless they had met regularly, these would have gone back to their old ways again. What works in French Equatorial Africa works here in America. To keep alive and growing as a Christian you need to meet with others for a Christian purpose, and He will be there. He is a gentleman and keeps his promises. 'Forsake not the assembling of yourselves together' . . . you cannot afford to."

What we say here, however, applies not only to attendance at public worship but to actual involvement in the life and work of the church. As the cells of the human body seem impelled to do the right thing at the right time, at the right place, in the right way, and life pushes forward, building, repairing, feeding, and casting aside, so the members of the body of Christ, the church, are part of an organism, constantly repairing itself and "building itself up in love." We minister to one another *in* the church in order that we may minister effectively, also, beyond the church.

### For Discussion

1. What, really, does the church mean to you—in what areas of your life have you been deeply affected by it and its teaching?
2. In what ways are you finding help and strength in the church for your everyday life and work?
3. Do you feel that you have found a satisfying and meaningful relationship in the church? Do you feel relevant to its life and work? Why?
4. In what ways do you feel you could speak out of your experience and vocation to help the church? Do you have a witness to the church?

*The pastor is not to
perform like a gladiator
before spectators but to
help equip every person
for his ministry.*

# CHAPTER VIII

# To Equip His People

In this mutual ministry to one another and in the arena of everyday life, where does the pastor fit? If the whole church is a ministry, how is the pastor's ministry different?

The pastor is not basically different from other persons. He is just as human, just as subject to fatigue, just as battered by problems, just as pressed for time, and just as beset by temptations. He should be thought of not as "superior man," but as "representative man."

The pastor is employed by the church for a specialized and very necessary ministry. He has undergone special training for that task. Because he has given a greater amount of thought to the cause of Christ in the world, he should have greater perspective and vision. He needs to be temperamentally fitted for the tremendous demands laid upon him.

It has been said that the pastor's work has greater "visibility." That is, it is apparent to all. In the circles of the church he has probably greater status, but he has no "corner" on God. His work just happens to be more specialized and intensive. He stands, as it were, on the godward side of the church.

Ecclesiastical organizations differ rather widely, and in these varying structures, the position, status, and authority of the ordained minister ranges from the hierarchical pattern, with its line of authority and command, to the pastor in the congregational system of government, who must be quite dependent upon his people. The purpose here is not to argue the merits or demerits of any system or government, but to portray the specialized ministry of the pastor in the local parish, in relation to his people.

Having used the word "minister" in its broader sense, we shall not here use the word as applying to the professional ministry. We choose the word "pastor" because it will be well understood, as referring to that specialized ministry in the local parish.

### "He Gave Some Pastors"

While not all "gifts of the spirit" are to be construed as qualifying one for this specialized ministry within the church, some are related directly to it. "And these were his gifts: some to be apostles, some prophets, some evangelists, some pastors and teachers, to equip God's people for work in his service, to the building up of the body of Christ" (Eph. 4:11-12, NEB). This passage describes, probably, better than any other, the peculiar work of the ordained minister, especially the pastor —"to equip God's people."

What equipment is needed for your ministry in the world? What kind of ministry must the pastor render to "equip" his people for witness?

First, of course, the Christian layman must be equipped to outlive and out-love the average man—not especially to out-argue, but to *outlive*. Without the backing of experience and practical conduct, it is of no use to waste time on explanations or argument. If the layman is to perform a significant ministry in the midst of life, in the framework of vocation, with problems buzzing around him, he must find a strength beyond himself.

He must also have the equipment of knowledge. Spiritual and biblical illiteracy is so common among present-day Christian laymen that it amounts to one of the major problems in the modern church. It is, to say the least, a poor advertisement for the church. Dr. J. H. Jowett told of seeing sandwich men walking through the streets of London looking thoroughly pinched and starved and wretched while their boards carried advertisements of "the best dinner in London."[1] Famished wretches were advertising sumptuous dinners! The lesson is obvious.

Laymen often need help in assessing their own abilities and limitations, strengths and weaknesses, and in seeing their proper relationships in the church or even in their vocation. Part of the necessary equipment of the Christian layman is to see himself clearly, to see his task imaginatively, and to gain a real sense of stewardship in the exercise of his own uniqueness and ability. He needs to see clearly those special opportunities which are his, made possible by his own peculiar set of circumstances and relationships. It is unfortunate if his conception of serving God is so narrow that it includes only certain limited ideas about "church work."

The pastoral ministry of the church must be such that it actually does equip people for the work of serving. Such a pastoral ministry must be *relevant* and *vital*. The idea that this is a career for which the main qualifications are a certain amount of organizing ability, tact and culture, being a good "mixer," and the facility of speech, with perhaps a decent level of piety, is hardly an adequate concept of the pastoral ministry. It isn't worth anything if it is not first and last and always a ministry beneath the Cross. It seems that we know something about almost everything except how to make Christians, how actually to win people. The pastoral ministry will do well to concentrate on training at this point.

Let us look at some of the areas of his work, all of them for the purpose of *helping* and *equipping you* as a *layman*.

## THE POWER OF WORSHIP

If worship is merely the "preliminaries" before a sermon, it probably isn't worth the time it takes. But what if it could accomplish such things as these:

---

[1]Related in the *Christian Herald*.

1. Replace fear, worry, and wasteful haste with calm self-possession.

2. Bring perspective, making great things look great and small things small, as they really are, correcting our scale of values.

3. Lead one to such candor in facing his own faults and sins, as to produce genuine repentance.

4. Lift one's devotion to a great cause, helping him see his hardship or trial in terms of God's character-producing purpose.

5. Rescue our fragmentary goodness from the self-consciousness and pharisaical righteousness to which it is so prone.

6. Humanize us, by a sense of affinity with other struggling people, in our efforts toward righteousness.

7. Produce a genuine sensitivity to the issues of our time and the needs of persons around us.

This is something of what worship ought to do. The Archbishop of Canterbury said, " 'To worship is to quicken the conscience by the holiness of God, to feed the mind with the truth of God, to purge the imagination by the beauty of God, to open the heart to the love of God, to devote the will to the purpose of God.' "[2] How could you express it better? For worship is discovering God's thoughts after him. Christians are *goal-people*. They *strive*. They *hunger*. They *thirst*. They *reach upward*. Someone said they have a "homing instinct."

Something should be said to laymen about the spirit of worship. Living in the midst of a secular and materialistic society, values get strangely and grossly warped. It would be a wonderful thing in the world if every man were compelled to go alone occasionally and face himself under God. Incidentally, most of the world's progress has come out of silence and meditation. If one's spirit is reverent and worshipful, he will discern the handiwork of God in the desert, the stream, the mountain, or the sea. If his spirit is thoughtless and careless, it will fail to discern God in the face of Jesus Christ himself.

There is always a danger of making worship merely a source

[2]See Ralph Sockman's *The Higher Happiness* (Nashville: Abingdon Press, 1950), p. 149.

of comfort or sedation, to go home to Sunday dinner with a comfortable complacence, having been calmed, feeling safe and secure. A ship in the harbor is safe, but that is not what ships are made for! They belong on the high sea, splitting the waves toward some sure destination. And worship should lead to fresh dedication, clarity of vision, a new sense of perspective and purpose. It ought to result in adventurous living.

Worship is of tremendous value and worth—until people begin to use it as an end in itself; then it becomes chaff. Paul Scherer said, "To rattle through it [worship] lifelessly, with no understanding of its scope and immensities; or on the other hand to clothe it with pious and pulpit manner, trying with false solemnity in ministerial, pontifical tones to 'talk like God' —this is to set up a barrier sometimes wholly insurmountable between earth and heaven, between the dryness of many days and the refreshment of still waters."[3] Worship is just as valuable and helpful as your attitude permits it to be. It dare not be an escape or refuge. At its best, it is a certain caliber of people, seeking, learning, and growing into maturity; reassessing, repenting, believing, praising, and moving out to new, high purpose.

The pastor is the leader of worship and the sermon is an integral part of it. The time he devotes to making this a vital spiritual experience is time well invested. Of course, the pastor himself should be a fervent worshiper, relieved of trivia, announcements, last-minute arrangements, and, if possible, all other distractions, so that the period of worship can be one of genuine spiritual quest in fellowship together under God.

### THE PREACHING MINISTRY

Every person needs in his heart a center of moral authority, a meaningful and valid scale of values, a sense of reverence for that which is important and perhaps a sense of humor for

---

[3]*For We Have This Treasure* (New York: Harper & Brothers, 1944), p. 140.

that which is trivial. Any true morality must grow out of religious convictions, and this does not consist in mere intellectual assent to some credal dogma or mere conformity to ritual and ceremony. It means a reverence for God that possesses one's whole life and commands a truly ethical behavior in the complex relationships one has to live in.

"Preaching," says Halford Luccock, "if it is to have adequate depth and height and breadth, must be theological preaching. Indeed, there is no other kind that is much more than a respectable embellishment of a comfortable life.

"This has been expressed with rugged force in the challenge to the church: 'If you have anything peculiarly Christian to say at this hour, for God's sake, say it! But if you can do nothing but mouth over the slogans of the street corner, or the usual banalities of the Chamber of Commerce, for God's sake, keep still!' Those are rough words, but so were many of the words of Paul, and of Jesus. If preaching is not basically theological, not the proclamation of a God who has acted, but merely an anthology of moral maxims, it soon comes to resemble the description of Matthew Arnold as 'a mournful evangelist who had somehow contrived to mislay his gospel.' "[4]

To be negative for a moment, it might be said of *some* preachers as it was said of some politicians, that "in these days they gas their audiences instead of electrifying them." Another wag put it this way: "Just because a man stands up in a pulpit and talks, he isn't necessarily delivering a prophetic sermon any more than if your cat had kittens in the oven, they would necessarily be biscuits."

God have pity upon the pastor who is so bound to what people think or so restricted by dictators in the pew that he can do nothing more than feed prejudices and minister to blind spots. He is of all men most miserable. And God pity, also, those blinded laymen who would so restrict, for they will

-----

[4] *In the Minister's Workshop* (Nashville: Abingdon-Cokesbury Press, 1944), p. 39.

deny their pulpits of red-blooded men of imagination, and produce a bunch of sissies who pass as spiritual leaders. Prophetic
preaching is made possible by laymen, as well as by preachers.
It is the outgrowth of the church's very life. A prophet has to
speak even the disturbing truth. And he has to say it when
and where it counts! The church needs it and the world about
us needs it. Prophetic preaching is the best insurance against
the subtle and insidiously evil forces of our time. Therefore,
let the man of God stand tall. Turn your pastor loose from banalities and superficialities. The church needs prophetic preaching in every generation.

There is always a certain penalty attached to courageous
preaching, and your pastor needs your support. "Nobody can
enter a fresh path," says Rufus Jones, "or bring a new vision
of the meaning of life, or reinterpret old truths—in short, nobody
can be a prophet—without arousing the suspicion and, sooner
or later, the bitter hatred of those who are the keepers and
guardians of the existing forms and traditions, and the path-
breaker must expect to see his old friends misunderstand him,
turn against him, and reproach him."[5] If you leave your pastor
standing alone, or even worse, suffering under your own criticism, you will have *betrayed* him—and God!

Why is all this being said to laymen? Because the white
light of truth is the perpetual hope of the church and of the
world, and the pastor who dares to preach prophetically to his
people week after week deserves the unqualified support and
encouragement of the red-blooded people who sit in the pews.

And remember, this is to result in action. It is not a per-
formance to be delivered for somebody's entertainment. Somewhere I heard a mischievous story about a new pastor who
had preached his first sermon, when a critical member of his
church, exceedingly overweight, waylaid him after the service.
"Not a bad beginning," the fellow said, patronizingly, "a bit too
scientific and modern, perhaps, but quite fair. Remember, Par-

---

[5]*Spiritual Energies* (New York: The Macmillan Co., 1922), pp. 58-59.

son, you must feed the sheep, feed the sheep." The new pastor
surveyed his bulky critic and replied, "My dear man, it is exercise you need, not food." Again the lesson is obvious!

In your pastor's preaching ministry he brings his greater
study and perspective on spiritual matters and lays it before
you to prepare you for your ministry in the arena of life every
day.

### The Ministry of Administration

One of the principal tasks of the modern pastor in the complex urban situation, especially, is that of administration, for the
ministry of many people must be coordinated and conserved,
conflicts must be avoided, and gaps must be filled. R. G. Le-
Tourneau said, "I think the preacher should be the sales man-
ager and the layman the salesman." An athlete said, "I think
the pastor should be like the captain of the team."

Out of a five-year study of theological education in the
United States and Canada came some important findings. Richard Niebuhr, chairman of the committee, reached the conclu-
sion that while the role and scope of work of the clergyman
has changed from time to time through history, the best present
concept is one of "pastoral director," and he has contributed
permanently to our thinking by portraying this administrative
role as valid and essential.[5]

This doesn't mean the pastor is a dictator, but it does mean
that he has a major responsibility in the correlation and guid-
ing of the work of many people. A church, like a ship, has to
have a pilot, and a ship, to run a straight course, can have
but one pilot and one helm or "steering wheel." There can't
be a steering wheel at every place in the pew. If a church is
to be effective, it has to have a leader who is at liberty to lead.
This assumes, however, that the pastor is wise enough and
broad-minded enough to provide situations in which the best
thinking, the perspective, and disciplines of many laymen can

---

[5]See *The Purpose of the Church and Its Ministry*, Harper, 1956.

be considered, and where planning for the total ministry of the church will arise from the dedicated hearts and imaginations of Christian laymen. After planning and distribution of responsibility, however, must come coordination, and this administrative work is an essential one indeed. Some people object to this, but it might be observed that the person who cannot lead and who will not follow invariably obstructs.

The "pastoral director" works *with* people, not *for* them. He is not the boss but the coach. He supports, guides, and encourages. His business is to "equip God's people for work in his service." Thus, your pastor serves you by helping you relate your own witness and work to that of many others.

<h2 style="text-align:center">The Ministry of Counseling</h2>

Always the pastor has had the work of a shepherd. That is really the meaning of the word "pastor." In years past the work of counseling and shepherding was less in the focus of attention than it is today. In the time of small, widely scattered congregations on the American frontier, with their occasional visit from an itinerant preacher, the situation was quite different from the larger church today in the urban center, with people living under great pressures.

Many thousands of people in recent years have turned to some professional counselor or competent pastor for the personal help they need. Many go to a pastor because of what he stands for and because they feel they will get, in the name of Christian love, a sympathetic hearing. (Then, of course, it is free.)

Counseling is a time-consuming task, and it seems to be growing all the time. Theological education is being geared to this and the training in this field is being upgraded and strengthened all the while. Special clinics are being held all over the country, with intensive training in actual counseling. It remains yet to be seen how far the pastoral ministry will go in this direction, but the need is very great.

The pastor is more than one who stands at the front of the sanctuary and delivers a sermon in general terms. He is frequently asked to help apply those principles in terms of specific needs, problems, and conditions. You may need such assistance yourself from time to time.

The pastor is not removed from the problems of daily living as some would suppose, for he shares the experiences of many people, stands beside them at their times of sorrow and bereavement, of sickness and death, and of newfound joy. He is constantly exposed to life at its ragged edges.

Many of the distraught people who come to your pastor will be from outside the church fellowship. Some will be pathological cases which he might be able to refer to some other professional person or to community resources. Many will bring personal or family problems which will require countless hours of his own time. Some will have difficulties of such a nature that he will have to call on the personal and group resources within the church to supply a healing influence. Thus his ministry augments your own and backs it up. You will draw upon his skill many times if you are encountering real needs in the people to whom you witness.

Do not, therefore, feel that your pastor lives in a different world and that he will not be understanding in personal problems. He should be prepared to bring to bear upon a specific situation the wider perspective of theological and philosophical training, of the discipline of psychology and sociology, and the benefit of vast observation. His shepherding role is indeed a vital one.

## COMMUNITY LEADER

If the local church is a responsible community organization, if it has a witness to bear, and a message to proclaim, one of its pastor's vital roles is representing it at every significant level of community life. Perhaps much of what he does will not result directly in "new members" but it is through him, perhaps, that the church reaches most significantly into the life of its community. If a pastor is thoughtful, vital, and courageous, he renders an inestimable service. His presence and example will add strength to what you attempt to do in your own witness as a layman.

In a sense, he may be considered also the "symbol" of the local church. It has been found by surveys and studies that a local church is best known through the name of its pastor after he has been there two to three years, and people will most often speak of the church as "Pastor Blank's church." More important than the denominational affiliation or the physical plant or the size of the congregation is the person and the presence of the pastor—his attitude, his outlook, his influence, his convictions. This fact has its advantages and its disadvantages, but whatever they may be, it is still true.

Here, then, are some of the areas in which the pastoral ministry is conducted. He is a valuable resource person to every witnessing layman as he reaches other people and indeed in the layman's own life and home.

## THE MINISTRY TO YOUR PASTOR

No one can be always giving. He must also receive. Your pastor is included in the mutual ministry of the church, in the giving-receiving fellowship. A pastor, like anyone else, is human. He has physical and emotional needs—the need to be appreciated and needed, the need for self-expression, the need to be frankly himself, rather than behaving in puppet fashion according to what is expected of him.

Since August, 1956, when a magazine article presented a rather exaggerated story on the "breakdown" of ministers, augmented about a year later by another magazine article, a great deal of discussion has taken place on the minister's mental health. Why all this interest and concern? A careful look indicates that there tends to be a conflict within the mind of the pastor today between his major values arising from his real sense of call, and the demand of daily duties—what is expected of him and his family. Deeper values tend to be postponed, while he is pulled toward the periphery, even to the superficial aspects of his work. So the character of his work declines. Shallow aspects take him over and build him in their own image. Some rather wide studies on the pastoral ministry show that he is absorbed in things which he considers are secondary. Being largely dependent upon the goodwill of people, financially and otherwise, he tends to become obligated to the very people to whom he owes an incisive kind of ministry. His greatest danger, therefore, is in becoming, really, a "false" person—not being really himself.

One thing the layman can do is to help set his pastor free for the real work to which he is called. He needs proper time for study and wide reading, if he is to be a prophetic preacher and intellectual leader. He needs the resources to make this possible. Many a church is robbing itself of a prophetic ministry by the excessive demands they place upon a pastor's time, thus making it impossible for him to grow intellectually.

Another element is adequate financial support. Most pastors are underpaid, with the exception of some parishes where alert laymen have lifted their sights and accepted their responsibilities. A wide survey shows that pastors are deeply concerned, at two points, especially: (1) in giving their children the kind of education commensurate with family ideals and high purposes, and (2) security at the time of retirement, especially housing. Many pastors live in parsonages and have little or no opportunity to provide for housing and income at the time of retirement.[6] Insecurity militates against a man's highest usefulness. Here you as a layman can help.

Laymen can strengthen and enhance the influence of their pastor, not only by their own esteem for him but by helping to extend his orbit of influence. They can call upon him to extend their own witness. They can present him in situations that are congenial and help him meet people on the right basis.

---

[6]Survey by Ministers Life and Casualty, 1962.

Laymen can absorb many small tasks which otherwise encroach upon a pastor's time for major responsibilities. Many pastors do much of their own typing, when a high school girl could often do it faster and probably better. Imagination on the part of laymen, even those who feel very limited in ability, would greatly enhance the work of the church and increase the usefulness of their pastor.

A layman can receive the pastor's ministry at vital points in his own life and home. Especially is this true of men. Some men (may their tribe decrease!) think of a pastor's work as belonging among women and children. A pastor needs the men too. He needs the heads of homes. He needs men of influence, leaders, thinking men—not just to pass the collection plate, but to enter into the thinking and planning and actually become involved in the tremendous work of the Kingdom.

Probably no honest man ever feels prepared, really, for the pastoral ministry, and times of discouragement are not unknown. The pastor's work is not so clear-cut that he can tell, at the end of each day, where he started and stopped. He cannot measure his success in statistics. It would be better measured in terms of spiritual maturity and personal growth. Franklin D. Elmer, Jr., probably expressed best this impossible, but gloriously challenging call which will not let a man go:

### THE PREACHER

He stands between the ever and the now—
A slender, tender,
Fragile coupling.

Through him pass the yearnings
Of the bruised and battered
Sons of earth—
The fervid hopes and prayers
Of cosmic neophytes
Perplexed and lost and lonely,
Clamoring for comfort
And hungering for courage
In the communion with the soul of souls.

Through him comes, returning,
That strange mysterious flood
Of power—
The stream of hope and healing,
The word of everlasting wisdom,
The hand outstretched . . .

And there is none but Christ
With whom to share his anguish
And he finds himself
Too slender
Too tender
Too fragile.

## FOR DISCUSSION

1. How have you seen the pastor's role and work? What does he do? What should he do?

2. If you were to list priorities among the many demands upon your pastor's time, what would you put first? _____ second? _____ third? _____ fourth? _____ etc.? _____

3. In what ways have you drawn upon your pastor's skills, knowledge or faith as you have performed your own ministry and witness?

4. In what ways have you needed your pastor's ministry in a personal way? How has he helped you or your family?

5. What steps should be taken in your church to lift the demand of minor things and let him concentrate on that which is most important?

*What you do in Christ's
spirit has value and meaning
far beyond the deed itself.*

# CHAPTER IX

# Your Ministry Goes On and On

Every intelligent and concerned Christian is keenly aware of the need for a massive and intensive witness in the world, at the points where it counts the most—in legislation, in international affairs, and at conference tables, where the destiny of mankind may be hanging in the balance. Your mind reaches back to the Treaty of Versailles, at the close of World War I, where the first seeds were planted for World War II, or you recall some of the conferences immediately following World War II and how the agreements reached have tremendous ramifications in the economic and political world since that time. The people of the world are so knit together now, in an interdependent and explosive proximity, that what happens in one part of the world seems to happen in all parts. It is as though we all lived on the same street.

To the thoughtful person this is simply overwhelming. What can one individual do, even though he may have considerable influence within his own small orbit! How can the Christian witness be borne out and beyond the limits of his own life and work? Much of the time we deal with results, not causes.

## A GREAT COMPANY OF BELIEVERS

Fortunately, you are not alone. You are part of a tremendous and vast company—a fellowship of mutual purpose which reaches around the world. We need to see two things clearly and with eyes of faith.

First, the individual's task, though small, is a significant and necessary part of the total Christian witness in the world, the total being made up of the millions of individual witnesses.

Second, we need to see the tremendous symbolic value of what an individual does, for the significance of the witness is not in a direct result only, but in its value as an object lessson, its illustrative meaning.

It is in something of this faith that we assert, "Your ministry goes on and on." If a man who works on an assembly line is doing a little bit on a job, never seeing the completion, we also ought to be willing to work at an unfinished task. You must have faith in the long process of God, and faith in his people as well. Even Jesus said, "My Father worketh hitherto, and I work" (John 5:17). Weymouth translates that, "My Father works unceasingly, and so do I."

As a Christian you are part of the biblical, historical, and international community of believers. The church is a divine continuum across the ages. The testimony of countless thousands who have gone before us is still ringing across the generations. That testimony is also continuing around the world, by humble people, in unsuspected places, as well as by outstanding Christian statesmen at the highest levels of business and government. What we need as Christians is a sense of solidarity, a faith in the power of truth as revealed by Christ and the power of his love wherever expressed.

### "Go" Means You

"Go ye into all the world," said Jesus. "Go, make disciples." This is our commission and our mandate as Christians. To go into the "world" and make disciples refers not only to geography and the nations of the world, but to every stratum and area of human society.

Upon whom is this kind of commandment binding? To whom was Jesus speaking? Who is to "go"—and how? Obviously he meant this commission to the entire body of believers. He was depending upon their unity of purpose, their cooperative spirit, and their intelligence to find the ways and means to do so. Yet his commandment comes also to every individual Christian, in every local church. These words were not addressed to a select few, but the individual can obey only as he sees himself and his own ministry in the framework of the whole ministry of the whole church.

The church as an institution cannot enter the marketplace or business or politics except as it does so through chosen individuals who are prepared and trained for their task. But if the whole church is a ministry now gathered together for worship, now dispersed into the marketplace, the shop, and the office, then obviously the church is going by its representatives into countless areas where the Christian witness takes place.

The nub of the question is whether the individuals who go are fit witnesses, whether they have strength of character, knowledge of the gospel, whether they are filled with the love of God and motivated to Christian witness. Are laymen properly equipped for this ministry in the context of their own vocation and life? Some of us feel that here is where we are most seriously falling short.

Perhaps we need to focus attention at a few points more specifically. (1) Every layman needs a sense of calling, an imaginative concept of what he can do. (2) He needs better training. The ministry of the church, and of the pastor in particular, should be geared more to this purpose. (3) He needs faith in the "management" that while he does his job at his place on the "assembly line," the whole process is in God's good hands and there will be a finished product. That is, he needs faith in the whole church and in God. (4) He needs to sense more clearly his relationship in the life and work of the church and the ministry of brethren to one another.

## YOUR MONEY GOES FOR YOU

Money is a medium of exchange, which passes freely from hand to hand. It is that currency which indicates the value of any particular article or property, and it, more or less, serves as a measurement of a person's skill or ability. In our way of life the scale of values is sometimes so warped that it is hardly a fair measurement, but nonetheless that is the meaning of money. Through money your strength, time, ability, and devotion can be expressed at the cutting edge of the Kingdom.

The principle of stewardship is far broader than money alone, but it *includes* money, the way we make it as well as the way we use it. The money we make represents, in large part, the way we expend our strength, energy, and time. The way we use it expresses our scale of values.

The first basic principle about the Christian faith is the *sovereignty of God*. He created us. He created the earth and all of it belongs to him. We are his by right of creation. If this is true—and it is—it demands of any honest person that life be lived accordingly.

The second principle about stewardship is *man's accountability*. Man is a creature, not creator. Man is a steward, not the owner. If he has dominion it was given to him. It all *belongs* to God. If man were the owner, he would owe no account to anybody, but he is *not* the owner.

The third principle is that man is to offer in *worship* and *reverence* his whole being. Worship is not an optional matter, therefore, but a normal and integral part of any honest person's life.

Worship must always be the offering of ourselves. The giving of money is as naturally and normally a part of genuine worship as the singing of a hymn. Some people think of it as a necessary nuisance, and the church as a beggar. It is not that, however much the church may need financial support. If you can imagine the church needing nothing in particular, you would still have a God-given obligation—and a *need*—to give. To reject the principle of stewardship is to reject the gospel itself. It is to reject the basic beliefs and attitudes of the Christian faith.

Your money is you, in a very real sense, and there is no higher act of worship than acknowledging the ownership and the divine providence of God by giving a regular portion of your income to his service. Some of us think that this cannot, in honesty, be less than one tenth of your income. It should be more! Giving should be out of the gratitude and overflow of the heart.

The principle of stewardship is the acceptance of God's entrustment to us, not something demanded of us or imposed upon us, but rather an honor which clothes us with dignity and purpose, and which gives meaning to life and vocation. God actually trusts us with things, facts, powers, ideas, ideals, raw materials, the water, the sky, the air, the sun, the minerals, the growing things, and even our own mental and physical powers. He trusts us with these as stewards. He trusts us with freedom, for he has placed in our hands some creative powers, the power to think, to build. He trusts us as trustees who deal with his property, including ourselves, our time, talent, possessions. He trusts us as friends, not servants blindly obeying that which we do not understand, but as friends who intelligently enter into his purpose in the world.

By the stewardship of money every layman can have a part in the ministry of Christ far beyond his own community or local church. If stewardship is practiced by the congregation as well as the individual, and it certainly should be, then to lay your offering on the plate in worship on a Sunday morning is to touch every continent and every phase of the many-sided work of God, from the mission field to the training of missionaries, from the leadership of the local church to the training of leaders on an international level.

The church has wisely established channels through which every Christian can obey the Great Commission and "go" into all the world. Time and money can be translated into printing presses, service centers, and classrooms, and like the loaves and fishes blessed by Jesus, it can multiply manyfold.

It is the privilege of every Christian to have a part in bringing light to people's hearts all over the world, of planting seeds which will germinate and grow, of helping to win people who will themselves become evangels and stewards. "When Bishop

Jas Thoburn, pioneer missionary, was en route to India, a businessman on shipboard said one day, 'Thoburn, you've got as much chance saving heathen of India as I have taking this teaspoon and using it to empty the Pacific Ocean.' The bishop's reply is a classic: 'My job is not so much to *use* a spoon as to *make* spoons.' "[1]

Somewhere I heard that only a few years ago all the Marquis wheat in the world could have been put into one small envelope, but now it is harvested each year in the millions of bushels. Perhaps you do not have wheat to feed thousands, but you can *plant* some!

Every cent you give, every moment you serve is an act of faith. Do you dare to invest yourself and your money? Your ministry will go on and on.

## Your Ministry Is Preserved

If you should attempt to serve God and perform your ministry completely independent of the fellowship of his people, and the disciplines of his church, it would likely be lost. In our time it appears glamorous to go "independent," to play upon, and even excite prejudices against the church. Some good people seem willing to conclude that the church is a lot of ecclesiastical machinery with too much overhead. They feel that there are more direct ways to get the work done. But the independent work often exploits the results of the regular church's faithful work across the years. It is something less than ethical to reflect upon the work of godly pastors who consistently serve their people, and upon local churches which have borne their witness faithfully for years in their communities.

Candor and honesty demand that we look realistically at the inefficiencies of the church as it is. We haven't been perfect. But equal candor and honesty will demand that we look at the waste and the dissipation of strength which sometimes occurs through irresponsible independent operations. Some extreme

---

[1]From *Pastor's Journal,* March 19, 1950.

cases must be classified as religious racketeering, inciting prejudices, and capitalizing upon every element of discontent.

I do not ask that the layman accept blindly and without question everything which is done in the church. I would ask that he take a long, honest look. Compare actual costs of operation, survey the work actually being done, its soundness, and its lasting quality. Most of all, let him ask himself, how long will this last? Can it go on and on? Will it be conserved?

Your own ministry is corroborated and strengthened by the ministry of others. The mutual helpfulness and fellowship of the church is a discipline and a guide. It is in the church that you learned the meaning of salvation. In the church you have been taught; in the church you have heard the preaching of the gospel; in the church you have seen Christian example; in the church you find your opportunity; and in the church your ministry will be preserved and carried forward. Those whom you reach will reach others. Those whom you teach will teach others.

## THE LARGER CHRISTIAN COMMUNITY

Someone told me the story of a visitor to Louisiana who was standing by the side of a bayou watching a shrimp lugger, laden with both passengers and produce, glide by. A native was standing by the side of the visitor watching with equal interest. The native finally turned to the visitor and remarked, "That lugger will go on down the bayou to Plaquemine, and—if they've a mind to—the passengers can get on a river steamer that'll take them straight to New Orleans. At New Orleans they can get a bigger steamer that'll take them across the Gulf; they can go to Mexico and South America and on and on. Why— you can go anywhere on this earth from a bayou!" A bayou is not a little puddle all alone. Neither should the local church be all alone. It opens to wider vistas.

A contrasting attitude is illustrated in a story told by H. Lee

Jones of a western rancher, newly arrived from the East, who noticed trout in the stream which traversed the property he had just acquired. Being unfamiliar with the nature of fish and ignorant of the law as well, he hit upon the idea of placing fine-mesh screens across the stream at both the upper and lower property lines. He wanted to be sure of having his fish and his fishing. Trout go upstream to spawn. None could enter his property from below; none could escape upstream to increase the trout population. His act resulted in fewer and fewer fish. When deliberately or through ignorance we center our attention solely upon ourselves, excluding the interests of others from our thinking and our acting, we discover to our dismay that, having believed in the self-enacted law of limitation, we have put it into operation against ourselves.[2] Do you get the lesson?

The sectarian spirit is always wrong. It is recognized by Christian leaders the world over that the great tragedy of Christendom in our time is its divided condition. Jesus prayed for the unity of his people, and he depended upon that as a witness to the world. There is no question that the ministry of the church in today's world is seriously hindered, for our division is a negation of the very message of Christ.

There are, of course, theological differences. We do not all see alike. Probably we never shall fully agree. But we can be tolerant and loving even while we hold to our convictions.

Commonly when the plea is made for magnanimity and generosity in religion, some think that it is a plea for a thinned-out faith and the surrender of personal convictions. On the contrary, it is really a plea to get down to the two basic convictions of all great religion. First, *one God!* This was the message of the great prophets proclaiming that across all human alienations and divisions there was *one* God, and every human being his child. "Have we not all one father?" cried the prophet. "Hath not one God created us? Why do we deal treacherously every

---

[2]*Good Business,* August, 1947.

man against his brother?" Across all lines of distinction that men have drawn we must ask, first of all and deepest of all: "Have we not all one father?"

The second basic conviction in great religion is the inestimable value of every personality. Some kinds of individualism break life up into fragments, but not this kind! Jesus' kind reaches beneath all divisions and lifts up every life, whether Jew or Greek, Scythian, barbarian, bond or free, saying, "You are a child of God, a person of infinite value." To have a religion that not only accentuates these differences but furnishes a whole new category of sectarianisms and partisanships is tragic.

C. E. Brown spoke of this from a conservative point of view: "The higher form of tolerance is that of one who has such a firm faith in the truth and in its final victory that he can afford to wait, to be patient, and to be courteous. Moreover, his heart is so full of love that he cannot help having a feeling of sympathy for all the struggles and mental conflicts of his fellow men."[3]

You as a layman, owe something to your own church—your local parish program, your state and area program, even the national and international outreach. You also owe something to the kingdom of God everywhere. The sectarian spirit is wrong just because it insists on fragmentation. God's work is one work in the interest of all mankind. The more we know his love the more we will give expression to this. At low tide there may be multitudes of separated pools along the shore. At high tide they are brought together and the little distinctions are lost in the splendid union of a powerful flood. It is that way when the love of God and man takes precedence in the hearts of Christian people; as the tide of love rises, distinctions disappear, and while people will not see or think exactly alike, they will rise together in a higher concern.

------

[3]*Gospel Trumpet,* February 10, 1940, (now *Vital Christianity*).

Someone has put it this way:

Each level of life must yield to a higher level:
    The clod of dirt must yield itself to produce grass.
    The grass must yield itself to the cow.
    The cow must yield herself to man.
    Man must yield himself to God.
    Even God yielded Himself to produce a kingdom. A
cross going up a hill taught us that there are some
things even God suffers for.

In the days of the apostles, the church came pretty close to being a little sectarian movement within Judaism. It was the magnanimous spirit of the apostles and the love of God in their hearts that caused them to reach a meeting of minds from time to time, especially as relating to the difference between the Jewish and Gentile culture, both of which were represented in the church in considerable numbers. On both sides they felt they had vital points and vigorously contended for them. Yet, Paul could later write to the Ephesians, saying, "He [Christ] is our peace, who hath made both one, and hath broken down the middle wall of partition between us" (Eph. 2:14).

If we as Christians, individually and together, are to fulfill the God-given mission to which we are called, we shall have to let the gospel speak in the midst of life and to all of life through *all* God's people. To be a Christian today means to be a "world Christian." Anything less is too little. We must find ways to work together in the local church, in the community, and out far beyond. The channels for such obedience are there. We need only to utilize them better.

## SYMBOLIC VALUE

Whatever is done in the spirit of Christ, with sincerity and integrity, has value vastly beyond the deed itself. It has *symbolic* value. It *illustrates* a law of life. It has the capacity to multiply itself in the hearts of other people.

Was this not true of Jesus? Who could measure the value and impact of his ministry in terms of the relatively few people he reached during his lifetime? Or who could measure its scope in terms of the limited geographical area in which he lived? Or its impact upon the cultures of the world by the type of people he directly influenced? When they nailed him on a cross on Calvary, it was not the end, but only the beginning, and he was, as someone has said, "set loose upon the world."

It is not too much to say that what you do sincerely in Christ's name and in his spirit will not stop there. It will go on and on. There is a difference between a "do-gooder," whose good deeds arise from his own emotional needs or his desire to dominate, and the true Christian, who by his deed unlocks a secret, expressing an eternal truth. His deed will be symbolic.

Out of World War II there came stories of unsurpassed courage and grandeur as well as those of cruelty. Take this letter from a German Christian, written to his English friend after the war had started: "With these lines I have to say farewell to you. We have to expect to be called for military service in Germany. What this means for men like ourselves who were blessed in these years of friendship and trust, by fellowship and love of Christians all over the world, cannot now be expressed in words . . . Now we have to go the way into darkness . . . And if the day comes when the light of God and His mercy will shine again upon our peoples and churches, then do remember, my dear friend, if I am still alive, that there is a friend of yours in whose heart all the spiritual heritage of thirteen years, does not fade away, and who will be ready for all the work of God after this time of great temptation." A letter like that can never die. Such an attitude has in it the seeds of the future.

Thousands of stories like that could be written and only eternity will reveal the power of Christian witness as it has been exercised in places high and low, in the limelight and in obscurity. We can believe that what one does sincerely in Christ's name and spirit *will not die.*

Bend, then, my brother, to your task. Dare to be transparently Christian! Dare to react in terms of a different scale of values. Dare to behave by the law of love, to light candles in people's hearts, to plant the seed for the future. "He that goeth forth and weepeth, bearing precious seed, shall doubtless come again with rejoicing, bringing his sheaves with him" (Ps. 126:6).

## FOR DISCUSSION

1. How do you see the work of your local church related to the worldwide work of the kingdom of God? What are the channels?

2. How do you see your own personal ministry related to the larger ministry of the church? Do you actually have much sense of relationship or do you feel pretty much alone?

3. In the financial program of your local church, what percentage of the money goes into the larger outreach of the church? Does it represent a real love for people and sense of mission?

4. Do you believe there is symbolic value in what one does in Christ's spirit? Can you give an example?

5. Do you feel that, as a result of this study, you can truly share in the ministry of Christ through his people? Do you plan to do so?